PLANNING A
PROFESSIONAL
CURRICULUM

PLANNING A
PROFESSIONAL
CURRICULUM

A Guide to Understanding Programme Design

by

Lawrence A. Fisher, Ph.D.
and
Cyril Levene, M.D.

The University of Calgary Press

© 1989 L. A. Fisher and C. Levene. All rights reserved.

ISBN 0-919813-21-6

The University of Calgary Press
2500 University Drive N.W.
Calgary, Alberta, Canada   T2N 1N4

Canadian Cataloguing in Publication Data

Fisher, Lawrence A., 1923
    Planning a professional curriculum

    Bibliography: p.
    Includes index.
    ISBN 0-919813-21-6

    1. Universities and colleges - Curricula. 2. Medical
colleges - Curricula. 3. Curriculum planning.
I. Levene, Cyril, 1926- II. Title.
LB2361-F57 1988   378.'1996   C88-091325-8

Cover design by Rhae Ann Bromley

Printed in Canada

TABLE OF CONTENTS

Chapter 13
Designing the evaluation of student performance 141

PREFACE

This book addresses itself to faculty members who are involved in the design, implementation, evaluation or modification of a curriculum leading to a professional qualification or degree. We assume that the reader is knowledgeable in one or more content areas, is perhaps now faced with the task of building anew or revising a course or collection of courses and feels somewhat unsure of the proper ways to proceed. In short, this book is for all professional faculty, since few of us escape the responsibilities and the challenges of engaging in curricular development.

In our discussions with colleagues many, if not all, of them have openly stated that despite their mastery of a given content area they often find themselves unable to put together in an efficient fashion all the pieces that constitute a full programme of studies. They feel most uncomfortable with procedures in curricular development and they are generally unaware that there are principles underlying such activities.

When a curriculum is to be developed in a new school, or an existing curriculum appears to be in need of a major overhaul, there is a temptation for faculty to plunge straight into the details of courses and hours of instruction in their deliberations. Before long they are faced with curricular choices that must be made, often with inadequate resources, and it becomes at once apparent that a strategy for dealing with such situations has not been developed. We have seen people concerned in such enterprises become lost in the confusion that followed, for they were attempting to deal with the minutiae of course content and with broad issues of educational philosophy or psychology at one and the same time. In addition, each local situation tends to be unique and to involve special factors not amenable to packaged plans and routines.

It is therefore not enough to provide faculty involved in curricular development with a ready-made plan to be followed step by step, like a cookbook. Instead, it is necessary that the basis for planning be made known and that it be understood by the planners, so as to permit the application of principles and procedures to different situations. In this way individual solutions to individual problems in curricular development are determined and facilitated.

In searching through the literature on curricular development of post-secondary programmes we have found only one other publication that deals with general strategies of curricular development at the post-secondary level, and in a manner helpful to faculty members who are involved in a specific project for a particular school. Its publication date is now almost ten years ago, and times have changed. There do exist some books on theoretical aspects of curricular development (e.g. Jonas 1978) but there has yet to appear a book to which one could turn for a summary of the sequential principles, and their modes of application, that should be followed in the design and operation of *professional* curricula.

Our book has been written primarily from our vantage point as members of the faculty of a comparatively new medical school with an experimental curriculum but we have included examples and illustrations from nursing and law as well, based on our experiences in working with members of those professions. We feel quite strongly that the principles and modes of procedure addressed in this book are relevant to curricular development and evaluation in *any* professional programme.

L. F.

C.L.

THIS BOOK HAS BEEN PUBLISHED WITH THE HELP OF A GRANT FROM THE ALBERTA FOUNDATION FOR THE LITERARY ARTS.

FOREWORD

This book approaches the general topic of curriculum planning in professional education. The development of a literature in curriculum planning has not been a general movement but has occurred piecemeal within the various professions. Take, for example, the development of new curricula within North American medical education. Thirty years ago, a small band of scholars in education ("educationists") at the University of Buffalo began studies of medical education in collaboration with some medical-school teachers who believed that "specialists in education" might be as helpful in their pursuit of excellence in medical education as were clinical specialists in *their* pursuit of excellence in medical care. Their studies, however, were only just beginning, and there were not sufficient data nor a broad enough experience to provide the background for a book of this type.

Early seminars, workshops and lectures in medical education, designed to help medical-school teachers become more proficient at their multi-faceted roles of curriculum-planning, teaching, assessing student performance, and participating in school-wide evaluation, had to rely on basic principles of education for the "content" of their sessions. That is, when participants in those pioneering sessions invariably asked for illustrations from their own world of medical education, the educationists at that time were unable to respond because they had not been involved in attempts to study the processes of teaching and learning in medical schools and had not been actively conducting research in medical education.

Thus, it would have been impossible to produce this book only thirty years ago. Even today, the achievement represented by this book could only have been accomplished by a few. The understanding of the dynamics of American and Canadian medical education, which is evident here, truly demonstrates a thorough grasp of the nuances and subtleties involved in all of the processes in which a medical school teacher is engaged. That understanding has not materialized out of the blue; indeed, such depth comes from the many years of investigation and consultation the authors have devoted to the world of medical education.

During these last three decades, the senior author has been a significant contributor to the growing body of knowledge and the systematic, critical review of medical education practices. In this time period, American medical education has become the object of scholarly investigation by a growing number of educationists who are devoting their full efforts to learning more about curriculum and instruction in the medical school and who are providing guidance and consultation to those who seek the improvement of medical education - both for themselves as individuals and for their institutions.

Starting in 1962, the Association of American Medical Colleges has conducted an Annual Conference on Research in Medical Education (RIME) with more than 500 original papers having been reported in that time. Several new journals in medical education have appeared, joining the *Journal of Medical Education* in publishing reports of research and development in medical education. The little band of educationists described by George Miller in *Educating Medical Teachers* has been augmented by a host of educationists, educational psychologists, and others trained in the disciplines supporting education. Indeed, two new organizations have appeared: the Society of Directors of Research in Medical Education, and the Generalists in Medical Education. In addition, medical specialties have formed organizations for the study of medical education: the Association for Surgical Education, and the Society of Teachers of Family Medicine, to name just two.

All of this activity in medical education, and to a varying degree within other professions, has served to generate much-needed data on teaching and learning in the respective professional schools. In turn, the people involved, aided by the newly acquired data, have provided leadership to a growing number of faculty in medical and other professional schools who are interested in and concerned about principles, practices and problems of professional education.

With all of this growth, however, there are still areas of glaring deficiency. For instance, most of the educational planning in American medical schools is lacking in thoughtful application of sound educational principles. Discussion of curriculum is more likely to consist of arguments and debates than to include open and thoughtful consideration of ideas. Myths and shibboleths are far more frequently invoked at curriculum committee meetings than are educational concepts and principles of learning. Convenience for faculty is usually of much higher priority than learning outcomes for students. Stated very simply, all too frequently curriculum planning is an emotional and political process rather than a logical and educational process.

The need for faculty to become knowledgeable in this very important area of educational planning is still with us, now perhaps more than ever. Moreover, it may be that the time is right for such efforts to be accelerated. After more than a decade of almost total disinterest in and inattention to problems of medical education, for example, there seems to be a growing ferment stimulated or furthered by the *Report of the Panel on the General Professional Education of the Physician*, issued by the Association of American Medical Colleges: the *GPEP Report*. For the first time since the early 1970s, medical school faculties seem to be turning again to what should be their major concern: the education and training of medical students to become physicians. The advantage today over the situation thirty years ago is that there now exists a rich resource of materials, experience and data to help new teachers become oriented to the educational component of their multi-faceted faculty role, and to help experienced teachers find better ways of fulfilling their educational obligations to the students.

Thus, the goals of improving professional education are well served by this book, which provides an excellent orientation for the novice and a rich reference for the veteran, along with many illustrations of ways in which curriculum planning can become more responsive to the needs of students, faculty and society. For those who want to learn more about teaching practices, for those who want to learn more about educational planning, for those who develop an interest in the scholarship of professional education, this book can be both a stimulus and a guide.

That this book can be published at all is evidence of a renewed interest in and concern for education now being expressed by a growing number of professional faculties. It is possible that this book might contribute to a shift in the classical identification that faculty in professional schools have with their respective disciplines. If, for example, one asks a medical faculty member, "What are you?" the response is, "I am a physiologist" or "I am a pediatrician." A follow-up question, "Yes, but what do you do?" usually gets the response, "I do research" or "I take care of patients." It is only if one persists with a third question that the response *may be* forthcoming: "I do teach students." This third-level identification has not been strong enough to generate deeper faculty commitment to the improvement of medical education.

This book by Fisher and Levene should serve to enhance the interest and alleviate the insecurity of new teachers, as well as reinforce the interest and restore the enthusiasm of experienced teachers, by providing them with references to both principles and practices in professional education, illustrated from the rich experience of the authors.

Stephen Abrahamson, Ph.D.
Professor and Chair, Department of Medical Education
Associate Dean for Medical Education
University of Southern California School of Medicine

Chapter 1

PLAN OF THE BOOK

The present chapter provides an overview of the contents of the book. These are arranged in the order we consider most useful to faculty setting out to replace an existing curriculum no longer considered adequate or to provide a curriculum where none yet exists. However, those who contemplate *some* change in an existing curriculum, but to a lesser degree than total replacement, may prefer to begin with the chapters or sections that seem most suited to their needs. Faculty who are simply curious about curricular change and would like to know something of the strategies underlying its successful achievement are invited to dip into the book at places where topics of particular interest to them are presented.

Chapters 2 and 3 can be viewed as preliminary. In Chapter 2 we survey the major factors, both internal and external, that contribute to the pressures for significant curricular change. We have chosen to write about them in terms of one type of professional school, the medical school. The survey illustrates that, although scientific endeavour is often pictured as the primary force producing curricular change, other factors such as faculty and student dissatisfaction or unrest strongly influence course design and even content. This has been true in the past, is true now, and will be so in the future. There is a need to examine the impact of such factors. Chapter 3 discusses the increasing involvement of individual faculty members in course design. This increasing involvement is a consequence of the demand, by those schools interested in upgrading their course of studies, for a commitment from their teaching faculty to engage in curricular renovation and improvement.

Chapters 4-8, which we consider the heart of the book, provide the basic concepts essential to an understanding of the planning process. The concepts are grouped into five themes which reflect the bodies of knowledge and research on which we have necessarily drawn. These themes are as follows: the broad context in which learning is to be fostered (Chapter 4); human learning: how it occurs, how it can be optimized and how it can be evaluated (Chapter 5); drawn from this last chapter, principles of instruction and of its organization (Chapter 6); evaluation: what it implies and what its components are (Chapter 7); and finally the necessary structure and organization of an educational institution, drawing from management and systems theory and including the nature of interactions among people in an organization (Chapter 8). This section concludes with the first steps of curricular change, which are organizational in nature.

With Chapter 9 we begin to apply the theories of the previous chapters to the curricular planning process. We look at the elements of curricular design (Chapter 9) and present various patterns of curricular organization, with their attendant advantages and drawbacks, that are used in institutions of higher learning today (Chapter 10).

Chapters 11 and 12 are concerned with the planning of instruction. This involves deciding on the design of courses and of smaller units of instruction (Chapter 11), and then using the selected designs to create an instructional blueprint (Chapter 12).

Evaluation of student performance forms the subject of Chapters 13 and 14. As in the case of instruction, deciding on a design for evaluation (Chapter 13) precedes construction of the blueprint (Chapter 14). Evaluation of the programme itself forms the subject of Chapters 15 and 16, with design (Chapter 15) again taking precedence over the blueprint (Chapter 16). Programme evaluation is concerned with the maintenance of a curriculum of high quality and proper focus through a process of periodic curricular review involving faculty and students.

The final chapter (Chapter 17) attempts to bring together the various strands of which this book is composed. In so doing it will emphasize the thesis that thoughtful preparatory decisions are necessary and must be taken before faculty energies are directed into the detail of course work, number and type of instructors, allocation of space and time, and sundry other matters.

We close this chapter on a note of caution. Curricular development, like research, is never completely finished. There are always further questions, issues and problems uncovered in the study of an ongoing curriculum that require fresh approaches to instruction and evaluation. Not only does course content change over the years as a consequence of continuing advances in knowledge, but faculty perceptions of what constitute appropriate learning and teaching techniques and what constitutes professional competence also undergo continual modification.

Chapter 2

ANTECEDENTS

The pace of curricular change in professional schools, although still slow, has quickened in the present century. The great variety of causes, and the different pacing, of this acceleration make it difficult to provide a single description applicable to schools of law, nursing, medicine, and so on. We shall therefore confine our attention to the medical curriculum and describe the main influences affecting it over the past hundred years, together with their effects in bringing that curriculum into its modern form.

Variable Content of Medical Curriculum

The development of the modern course of medical studies in Europe and North America shows strong evidence of variation in the scope and depth of intellectual challenge (Lippard 1974). At times the requirements for the M.D. degree or its equivalent were minimal; in some instances in the seventeenth and eighteenth-centuries the degree could be purchased for a fee. At other times the programmes of medical studies were long and arduous, with students flocking to those institutions which provided challenging lectures and broad experience. By the twentieth century there existed on both continents a number of schools affiliated with universities, together with a more numerous group that was free-standing and fee-supported: the so-called proprietary schools.

Medical Schools Investigated

In North America at the start of the twentieth century the requirements for the degree seemed so variable, and the quality of medical practice so uneven, that an investigation of existing medical schools in the U.S.A. and

Canada was carried out under the aegis of the Carnegie Foundation for the Advancement of Education. The Foundation selected Dr. Abraham Flexner, a non-medical educator, as its investigator. Flexner visited each medical school, established minimal criteria of adequate programming and then published his report (Flexner 1910). It contained a straightforward commentary on each of the schools visited and a pointed discussion on the quality of medical education in general.

The impact of the report was such that over half of the total number of proprietary medical schools in the U.S.A. and Canada closed their doors. Of those schools that remained open, many quickly sought the scientific and *Major* financial support of the nearest university. The greatest *consequence* educational consequence of Flexner's report was the *of* reconstruction of the medical curriculum in all schools. *report* There was, henceforth, a strong emphasis on those biological sciences viewed as contributing directly to clinical understanding and practice. In addition, improved clinical experiences were now provided for senior students in hospitals and clinics under the jurisdiction of the university. Some of these hospitals became identified as "teaching" hospitals; in them it was expected not only that students would be tolerated in clinical settings but also that the attending staff of those hospitals would take their academic appointments seriously. The curricula that emerged from this period of reform typically had two to four years of basic science instruction followed by two years of clinical instruction leading to the M.D. degree or its equivalent.

Internal Problems

In this way the medical schools continued until the late 1950s. By this time medical faculties were often at loggerheads over who should have possession of the available time in the curriculum. Each department sought more assigned time and each developed a rationale in support of the additional time that it demanded. Furthermore, basic science departments had grown in number and in strength and had found increased rewards in developing strong research and graduate programmes in their own disciplines. The burgeoning of basic science knowledge made it seem imperative to each department that *it* receive greater recognition in the general medical school curriculum. There was continual manoeuvring through changes in assigned time based on the strength of personality of the department head or on his ability to coerce the administration into giving his department more time in the curriculum. The problems appeared insoluble.

A small medical school, Western Reserve University, attempted a solution to these problems (Ham 1962). In examining their courses the faculty discovered that there was little co-ordination of the content between different disciplines and that many duplications and omissions could be demonstrated. The solution appeared to lie in a reorganization of the course

First attempt at solution of studies that would increase the efficiency of teaching, in the first place by integration of disciplines. It also seemed pedagogically sound to integrate the content of the basic and clinical science courses so that the students, through learning by association, would retain what they learned for a longer time than had previously been the case. Clinical instruction would be the anchor for basic science material.

As this required a complete change in course structure it was decided to build the curriculum around courses focussed on body-systems such as the urinary system and the cardiovascular system. In each of these courses the related content of anatomy, paediatrics, biochemistry, surgery, and those other clinical and basic medical sciences which contributed to an understanding of a particular body-system, would be taught while the students were investigating some clinical problems presented by patients with disorders of that system. The task of reconstructing the curriculum on this new principle took several years and was pursued against strong opposition. No fewer than six department heads left the medical school, most for other reasons but certainly some because they could not in all conscience countenance such a radical change in curricular organization. Still, the faculty was able to accomplish the task and introduce the new courses.

After several years of implementation, involving changes and modifications of the original plan, the new scheme came to be regarded as a qualified success even by other schools, which sent faculty to study the new

Diffusion of ideas programme at Western Reserve. The idea spread widely and it is now the case that in Canada and the United States it is no longer difficult to find a medical school that includes, in the first two years of medical studies, at least one integrated course with a similar organization around some grouping of the basic medical disciplines. To be sure, there are schools that, while recognizing the necessity of making their non-clinical instruction more effective, have simply initiated short courses called "clinical correlations" during the years devoted to the basic sciences. In so doing they, also, are attempting to relate the basic medical sciences more directly to the clinical sciences and thereby meet the students' demand for "relevance".

Student-inspired Reforms

The impact of the student unrest of the 1960s had equally pervasive consequences (Schwab 1969). First of all, and again in the name of relevance, there was a demand for greater clinical experience during the years of attendance at medical school. This was met by increasing the instruction given at affiliated or wholly owned teaching hospitals. Community hospitals were encouraged to give space and time to the instruction of medical students, thereby broadening the experience of students in the types of medical care provided. Practitioners were persuaded to take students into their own offices and to act as preceptors for them in clinical experiences related to their current classroom studies.

More clinical experience

Secondly, students reacted strongly against animal experimentation and laboratory demonstrations in general. Most American medical educators active in the 1960s will remember the strong reaction of students to animal sacrifice. It used to be that students would jeer at fellow students who failed to "complete" their experiments by sacrifice of the animals and instead, by leaving the laboratory, passed this responsibility on to the laboratory staff. By 1970, students were openly challenging laboratory instructors who employed animals needlessly, in the opinion of these students, in experiments intended to demonstrate facts already incorporated in their textbooks or available in the recent literature. Students also made very clear to their instructors that, when required to perform or observe animal experiments, they then wanted to go on and see how the new knowledge gained from such experiments could be applied to the problems of human patients. By 1980 the faculty response had settled to a decrease in the number of laboratory sessions in which students performed their own experiments, together with the replacement of others by group discussions based on observation of experiments performed once by the instructor.

Modified laboratory exercises

Thirdly, there developed an increasing emphasis on the *process* of medicine: the nature of medical problem solving or clinical reasoning, and how the ability to reason clinically was acquired. The process itself, seen as a unifying element in the medical school curriculum, was introduced as the common theme to be followed in moving from course to course and from the study of one clinical specialty to another (Feinstein 1967; Cutler 1985).

Emphasis on process

Attention to Learning and Instruction

Attempts were also made, and continue to be made, to provide better support for learning. Schools sought assistance in curricular planning and in course design. They became interested in the methods and quality of their own instruction and they studied their own deficiencies (Miller 1980).

Short programmes were offered to faculty who wished to improve their instructional techniques (Miller 1961; Hubbard 1971). Examinations were upgraded, again with educational technicians as guides, and assessment of students was investigated as an instructional process in its own right.

During the 1960s and 1970s attempts were made to capitalize on the current emphasis on individualized instruction in higher education (Skinner 1968). Learning resource centres were established and funded for this *Self-instruction* purpose. In order to encourage students to use these centres elective time was greatly increased; the extra time also enabled students to pursue selected topics in depth and permitted them to explore vistas not usually open to them in the regular curriculum. At the present time almost all medical schools have a large catalogue of electives which attract not only local students but those from other medical schools as well. Besides this emphasis on the individual, increased use was made of small-group teaching as a mode of instruction apposite to an understanding of the complicated relationships and complex concepts that typify medical knowledge.

A few medical schools experimented with shortened elapsed time for medical studies, for example three-year as opposed to four-year curricula. In the United States a number of three-year *programmes* were begun in *3-year curricula* response to pressure from state legislatures. These programmes have not fared well against four-year programmes on the same premises, for under pressure from their own faculties almost all of the three-year programmes have been returned to the more usual four-year structure. In Canada two schools, those of McMaster University and the University of Calgary, continue to offer three-year curricula and continue to meet accreditation requirements without question. The point is worth making that a careful study of the curricula of many four-year medical schools shows them to be not too far removed from the three-year structure, for their fourth year is devoted almost exclusively to student electives, producing in effect a 3 + 1 program.

Student dissatisfaction with what they regarded as the pointlessly competitive atmosphere for high grades in medical schools resulted in a significant change of emphasis in the goals of learning. More importance was *Competence v. competition* given to the achievement of carefully defined increases in professional competence, and less to the comparison of a student's grades with those of his classmates. Some schools went to a Pass/Fail system of recording student performance on tests in order to decrease the level of competition. Some schools required that all students meet a specified level of performance on examinations: the so-called "criterion-referenced" approach to evaluation of student performance. This did away with the arbitrary plan of consistently failing a set percentage (say 5 per cent or 10 per cent) of each class regardless of total class performance; such a plan requires for its justification the supporting assumption that classes be equal in ability and performance from year to year, an assumption that can be met only by very large classes.

The Person as Well as the Disease

There has also been a continuing movement to legitimize the behavioural sciences such as psychology, sociology and communication as essential components of the medical curriculum. This movement was a response to the recognition that while physicians had learned much about treating *disease*, particularly organic disease, they still had some distance to go in learning to treat *illness*, the patient-perceived state that usually accompanies disease but can exist in the absence of demonstrable disease. The introduction of the behavioural sciences into the medical school curriculum has not always been successful; nor has it always been tactful, as the sponsors have on occasion neglected to orient themselves to the roles of physicians, to analyze the needs of physicians arising from those roles, or to translate those needs into course objectives toward which they could teach. Still, the previously mentioned emphasis on process has provided a continuing opportunity for the introduction of "soft science" concepts into medical curricula.

New Directions

In the late 1970s and early 1980s there were several new movements in medical education. The emphasis on problem-solving as an organizing theme for a curriculum had been developed earlier by McMaster University Faculty of Medicine and this was now adopted by two other schools: the University of Newcastle in New South Wales, Australia, and Southern Illinois University in the United States. These two schools have provided national and international leadership to other medical schools interested in developing such a curriculum.

As medical schools found it increasingly difficult to obtain funding for university-based hospitals they were driven to seek affiliation with community and regional hospitals so that these might serve as educational bases for medical school programmes. This movement towards community institutions has been endorsed by the World Health Organization, which has organized the newer schools using such a community affiliation into a world-wide group that meets on a regular basis to share experiences and problems.

In the field of evaluation of student performance medical schools are now turning away from patient management problems and complex clinical simulations to the development of single-task clinical situations in which the student is required to demonstrate specific skills in a prescribed time of only a few minutes' duration. This change in emphasis in evaluation was brought about by the results of studies on the design and use of patient management problems which demonstrated their low reliability, and hence their low predictive ability, in the evaluation of clinical problem-solving. The First Cambridge Conference in medical education held in 1984 (Wakeford 1985), at which these studies were presented and discussed, has had an interesting impact on the evaluation of student performance in medical schools, and its influence will continue to grow.

Other trends in medical education are still to appear on the horizon. Relatively new medical sub-disciplines such as geriatrics and medical genetics have made permanent places for themselves in the contemporary medical school curriculum, and other fields are placing continual pressure on the loaded curriculum.

Chapter 3

THE INSTRUCTOR

The changing concept of the curriculum has been parallelled by a change in the role of the faculty member in the design and implementation of the curriculum. At the turn of the century the department head decided what

Instructor as servant

was to be taught, by whom, by what methods, and at which times, the total allocation of time for this and every other discipline having been decided by the heads of departments acting as a group. The faculty member,
on the other hand, was expected to obey with little question the orders relayed to him[1] from the departmental office: he was to give the lectures on topic X; he and a colleague were to supervise the related practical or laboratory sessions, while a third colleague was to arrange clinical activities involving students in the same area. Senior members of the department were given the task of assisting the department head in setting and marking examination papers. All of these tasks were imposed at the absolute discretion of the department head and were carried out under his direct supervision. In many ways the members of a department were the servants of the department head and their part in the curriculum was to do as they were told. If a junior member of the department had any ideas to suggest he did so at his peril, for such encroachment on the prerogatives of the departmental head was anything but welcome.

Over the years it became increasingly recognized by all faculty members, including department heads, that this system produced several problems. It ignored many potentially valuable contributions to the cur-

Instructor as participant

riculum; it concentrated power unduly; and it institutionalized resistance to change. With the growing demand for more effective departmental administration, including the paperwork, it was inevitable that decision

11

making in instruction and course design would eventually be distributed among the department members. Thus the department head came to be regarded as the foremost among equals and as the spokesman for, and executive of, departmental consensus rather than autocratic fiat.

With the diffusion of responsibility for the educational programme throughout the department, individual members began to recognize that they now had significant opportunities for leadership in instructional design *As leader* and implementation. Some of them sought assistance, most often among members of their own discipline, in learning the rudiments of these tasks; some did not. Regardless of individual reaction they were generally quick to assume the prerogatives of course management; but designing and offering a course can be troublesome without a command of the principles and practices of course construction.

Parallel to the broadening of the administrative base within the department, there developed a movement to assign individual responsibilities on the basis of demonstrated talent rather than by administrative decree. Thus, it is now accepted that while a *department* survives in an academic setting only by paying equal attention to research, teaching, and service of some kind, particularly in a professional school, this balance need not be reflected in the assigned responsibilities of each and every *member* of the department. Currently, the most common formula for individual survival in an academic career is that a faculty member must be proficient in two of the three legs of the academic stool and also enjoy a national and international reputation in one of them. Both national and international are mentioned because a solid reputation at the national level is not necessarily concomitant with an international reputation.

A faculty member who claims proficiency in teaching as one of his special competencies soon finds that it is rather proficiency in educational matters that is demanded, for the role of educator is more than that of teacher *Teacher* or instructor. As a teacher, one can provide instruction *as* using little more than the basic skills of lecturing, lead*educator* ing small group discussion and following a text outline. As an educator, however, one must know the subject-matter with enough intimacy to provide impromptu alternative explanations and descriptions of phenomena, concepts and principles, so that students having difficulty in understanding the basics of a discipline are provided with alternative intellectual maps by which to navigate through course content. One must know one's students, too: what they bring to class by way of knowledge, interests, skills; what they find most difficult and most easy in working through a course; and what prior experience they have had that shows some connection with the course being studied at the time. One must also know oneself; this implies that the educator must be acutely aware of the skills, knowledge and interests that he can bring to bear on the course content, in order to give the student as much help as possible in developing proficiency in the subject. In summary, to be an effective educator one must continuously keep abreast of current research in the field of expertise, inform oneself of characteristics of the current students, and be aware of the often subtle personal changes that take place as one progresses in the role of educator. We shall explore in successive chapters some of the attributes that define an effective educator.

Putting the student first There has been another change in academic focus which affects the role of the educator in professional schools. The work in programmed instruction and in computer-assisted and computer-managed learning in post-secondary institutions has resulted in an altered emphasis in educational design and instruction from the faculty member as teacher to the student as learner. The challenge is no longer just to lecture, with the student learning passively by listening to or watching the instructor, but to construct situations that stimulate or obligate the student to learn, prompting him to learn on his own initiative by providing the challenges and the facilities to meet those challenges. Put another way, the faculty member is freed from the obsession with his own performance; in its place he is given the opportunity of creating innovative methods for helping students to learn, and the scope to conduct research into methods of improving the learning/teaching situation for a range of curricular purposes (Cantor 1953; Miller 1980).

Broader vision of a discipline Over the years the advantages of interdisciplinary research have been making themselves felt, and the existence of funded interdisciplinary research groups has tended to undermine the cohesiveness of the classical departments. The research function has begun to break free of departmental labels. Faculty members professing a discipline no longer confine themselves to the concepts and techniques classically associated with their own discipline. Researchers from different disciplines find themselves arriving in the same intellectual territory from different bases. This in turn has led to a broadening of the conceptual bases of individual faculty members and to a growing demand for integrated teaching, with representatives from different disciplines planning together to teach together. To be a successful educator in a professional school today one must not only feel intellectually comfortable with one's own discipline but also be more than superficially acquainted with a number of others.

Faculty members are now aware that they can have a variety of roles to play in the curriculum, depending on the type of local curriculum, the way the administrative apparatus is organized, the degree of instructional freedom that is allowed and the strength of their own commitment to the educational programme. There is a minimum of teaching that each faculty member must do and there is a maximum beyond which existing constraints make it inadvisable for him to go, but within these limits there is considerable scope for the faculty member to try out his enthusiasms, his creativity, and his commitment to research, in medical education. In order to help him meet these opportunities in an intelligent manner we shall turn to a consideration of learning as an individual and as a group process, the topic of the next few chapters.

1.   We use "he", "him" and "his" for both genders throughout this book, partly as a matter of convention and partly because the alternatives would be so clumsy as to distract the reader.

Chapter 4

THE CONTEXT OF LEARNING

On occasion one wonders why so much time seems to be spent, in educational treatises, in talking about learning. After all, we learn quite well; how otherwise could we survive in our daily living? While we learn from life we are nonetheless unconscious of the cost of learning and hardly aware of the magnitude of the returns on our investment of time, energy and close attention. We *are* aware, however, that we meet with varying degrees of success in learning and that there seem to be a number of different factors involved in the process. In formal learning we expect that our instructors will be aware of these factors and will manipulate them to our advantage when we are trying to learn. One factor of some importance, though too often it receives scant attention, is the environment or context of learning. It has several components: a physical environment, a psychological environment, a cognitive environment and a sociological environment. These will be considered in turn, with emphasis on the latter.

Physical Environment

Room structure, temperature, air, lighting, acoustics, these aspects of the physical environment of learning are seldom neutral in their impact. They help or they hinder learning, so that as faculty members planning for learning we should plan for as much control of these factors as possible in our curricular design and implementation. This means exerting some control when the teaching facilities are being designed and built, or redesigned and altered, since buildings seem so permanent. The nuances of architectural design and interior decoration are outside the scope of this book; suffice it to say that the minimal requirement for each student is a study area free of distraction and conducive to focussed attention, with classroom and professional settings that provide an identifiable learning space guaranteeing preceptor-student discussion in privacy.

Psychological Environment

The efficacy of the curriculum is also affected by the psychological environment for learning. The individual backgrounds of the instructor and of the students produce a contextual effect on learning, helpful in some ways and detrimental in others, regardless of course content.

If we look first at the students, we should know in some detail the knowledge, attitudes and skills that each student brings to his learning. A course of studies intended to promote efficient learning should build on the strengths that students bring to their studies and compensate for the weaknesses in their backgrounds. We shall have more to say about this in a later section of the book concerned with course design. In like manner we should be cognizant of the particularities of the instructors who will be implementing the curriculum. They, too, have individual backgrounds of knowledge, attitudes and skills on which they must rely when designing courses and offering instruction to students. Instructors, like students, have strengths and weaknesses that have to be taken into account in the planning process.

Cognitive Environment

The subject matter or discipline that the students are asked to learn is a significant contextual factor. Each discipline has its own structure, with terms and concepts, principles and relationships, that are more or less specific to that discipline. The degree to which the fundamental ideas of a discipline are capable of being derived from other bodies of knowledge already known to the students determines the extent to which the new discipline is "teachable". A discipline is readily teachable if the student can build his learning of it on ideas acquired previously and recalled into consciousness early in his new studies. It is not only the content of a discipline that provides context, however; equally influential on the process of learning are the modes of exposition and demonstration used in that discipline. When concepts are tied together derivatively, then a close attention to the chaining of ideas is important in learning what is required. On the other hand, if there are few derivative relationships then the learning must be accomplished by an appeal to analogy or simile in developing comprehension.

Internal Sociological Environment

Learning has also a sociological environment, both internal and external. In regard to the internal context or climate of learning, there are sociological factors in each teaching and learning situation that affect the whole process. The instructor is expected to perform certain tasks in carrying out his responsibilities as a teacher. If he chooses not to do so, then he will be perceived by his students as not adequate to the task unless it is made quite clear to them why the normal expectations are being set aside. Similarly the students are expected to perform certain tasks when involved in learning, and students who do not do so are considered unresponsive or uncooperative.

External Sociological Environment

The external sociological environment refers to those forces in society which impinge on the professional school and its programme. It merits a more extended consideration here and we shall use the medical school as our example to illustrate the issues involved.

Degree of Autonomy

Medical schools around the world enjoy varying degrees of autonomy: some are free-standing proprietary schools; some are sponsored by government departments or ministries; most are affiliated with, or form an integral part of, a university. Each arrangement has its own advantages and drawbacks.

Regarding the merits of being part of a university structure, there is first of all the proximity of a variety of academic resources: academic staff, libraries, laboratories, all established and functioning on a larger scale *As part* within the total university. This broad context for the *of a* medical school is seen by some as a safeguard against *university* the school becoming what has been emotionally labelled a "trade school". Academic standards in the rest of the university are thought to act as a counterweight offsetting the tendency of clinical service work to "erode" the academic standing of the medical faculty. The university is assumed to provide encouragement as well as opportunity for medical and non-medical scientists and teachers to work together in research and in educational planning and implementation. Another advantage is that newer approaches to the medical curriculum, such as development of a behavioural science component, can benefit from the staff already present on the university campus who are experienced in teaching in those areas that have traditionally been absent from medical curricula. Finally there are the prestige and reputation of the university on which the medical school can draw, an important factor in the development of funding for educational and research programmes.

The disadvantages of being tied to a university are well known. The medical school is subject to the rules and regulations of the university, so that its own purposes and goals are subservient to those of the university. The university requires a particular organization of the school and of its courses, and a particular format for its examination results. Criteria for appointment and promotion of medical faculty and staff, and the procedures to be followed, must conform to those of the general university. A commitment of faculty time is required to the university's committee system. The medical school is obliged to mount graduate programmes that are non-clinical and even non-medical, to offer "service" courses to students of other faculties, and to provide continuing education to graduates of medical schools as part of the university's responsibility to professional development.

On the other hand, being free of the university structure provides certain opportunities. Given the conditions that always accompany the granting of funds, the medical school is able to chart its own course to meet its own goals without, as a prior commitment, having to *As autonomous school* take into account its expected contribution to the university as a whole. It need not be concerned with any incompatibility between its own goals and those of the university. It is free to solicit funds directly from external sources, in its own particular manner, given the requirements of government departments and ministries as sources of funds. The disadvantages of being independent of university affiliation have mainly to do with the difficulty of establishing an intellectual reputation that will permit the medical school to compete with the universities for research funds and for essential non-clinical staff.

Relationship with the Community

Part of the context of the medical school is the nature of its relationship with the community in which it finds itself. The school will want to provide a practical experience for its graduates; to do so, it must have access to hospitals, clinics and other agencies in the community providing for the health of its citizens. In moving into the community, however, the medical school must think through the nature of its intervention very carefully, for this in part determines the nature of the graduating student.

How might this intervention be conceived by the medical school and by the community? The medical school might consider itself to be essentially an academic centre, seeking community health facilities in order to enlarge its academic functions of teaching and research. The prime beneficiary of intervention is to be the medical school, with secondary benefits accruing to the community as byproducts of faculty and student involvement. Alternatively the school might regard itself as essentially part of the health care system offering educational, research and exemplary service activities as ways to maintain and improve that system. The prime beneficiary of the school's use of community health facilities is then to be the community, with secondary benefit to academic activities.

These two approaches are not in any way considered as being mutually exclusive, for there is always a mix. The important decision is not which one to choose but where to put the emphasis. The absence of a clear decision on the primary role of the institution leads to a situation in which other decisions vitally affecting the progress of the school are, by default, left to manipulation by the administration for its own ends, subject only to the pressure that will be exerted by the power structure of the faculty either with, or more likely without, prior attempt at faculty consensus.

Relationship with Local Practitioners

A particularly intricate task in recent times for a new medical school has been obtaining the support of sufficient members of the medical and other health professions. Some physicians tend to distrust the establishment of a *Their concerns* medical school in their immediate community, and their concerns deserve special attention. One concern is competition for patients, whether from faculty physicians at the university medical centre with its superb facilities and the resources enabling its medical staff to devote more time to each patient, or from recent graduates of the school with their modern training and up-to-the-minute knowledge. Such "unfair" competition may very well affect the practices of established physicians and perhaps their incomes. Further uneasiness is engendered by the anticipated development of hospital care in the region into a three-level system, with tertiary care captured and retained by medical school clinicians. The rest of the profession consisting of the practitioners already established in the community will then, it is feared, be relegated to the primary and perhaps some secondary care levels. It is also found that, at first, medical practitioners who agree to accept students into their offices for part of their clinical training often worry that the intellectual demands of the medical students of today will be overpowering and that student assessment of the quality of medical care provided by the practitioners will be overly critical.

All of these apprehensions coexist with expectations of specific benefits that will accrue to practitioners in the region from the existence of the medical school. These typically centre about the educational role of the *Their expectations* school. Practitioners expect the school to provide them with programmes in continuing education that will enable them to update their practice of medicine and improve its quality; and they expect the medical school, as a matter of course, to seek their counsel in setting up these programmes. They also look to the school to provide short programmes designed to develop their skills and attitudes as preceptors for the medical students assigned to them. They anticipate, as an important result of these programmes, a progressively influential role for their group in the educational programme at all levels, a role in which they will come to feel increasingly comfortable.

Societal Expectations for Graduates

There are also the expectations of society in general for graduates of medical schools. The public is becoming more aware of the length and intensity of the medical training that is required for the competent practice of

A caring attitude

medicine. At the same time it perceives the graduates of former years, who are its current medical advisers, as having sacrificed a listening and caring attitude in order to meet the demands of mastering a greatly increasing body of knowledge, much of which they suspect may not be essential. Although the public may agree that medical schools continue to emphasize knowledge, it demands that they now produce graduates as much interested in, and capable of, helping people as they are committed to treating diseases scientifically. Patients have also become more knowledgeable about medicine, demanding that they be involved in decisions regarding diagnostic and therapeutic procedures to which they may be subjected Patients do

Sharing decisions

not want to become involved in the purely medical aspect of these decisions, which is a matter of technical information and professional expertise. Rather, they wish to take part in deciding whether the benefits to be obtained from those procedures are going to be worth the distress, discomfort, inconvenience, embarrassment or financial sacrifice that will be required of them. These are matters in which the judgement of the patient is at least as important as that of the physician.

Although less true today than in the past, the community also expects physicians in their midst to assume some leadership responsibilities within the community. This is particularly the case in those communities in which

Providing community leadership

the physician constitutes one of the few intellectual resources of the community. If the medical school takes this expectation seriously, then young physicians will be encouraged to make themselves familiar with the general needs of the society of which they are a part (Rogers 1980).

While we have been considering the external sociological context of the medical school the non-medical reader will doubtless have called to mind analogous situations in his own profession. It is not so much the nature of the problems that differs as it is the circumstances of their application to the different professions.

In summary, there are many factors external to the sessions organized as a course, or to the collection of courses organized to form a curriculum, that form the context of learning.

Chapter 5

THE PROCESS OF LEARNING

Introduction

Faculty members often ask, "What is known about how post-secondary students learn?" The answer to this simple question turns out to be complex. Why so? Research has been directed into many individual facets of the subject such as role learning, problem solving, decision making, verbal learning, to name a few. As a result, each type of learning is covered by one, or more than one, discrete theory. On the other hand the applicability of any one theory to all aspects of learning has in no case been established. Furthermore, because of the different interests and emphases of different psychologists, the research on learning variables carried out by one investigator is considered almost irrelevant by another. This is especially true where experiments on learning have been conducted under strict laboratory conditions, far removed from the interaction of the many variables found in most classroom settings (Hilgard & Bower 1981). In sum, the difficulty in describing adequately how post-secondary students learn is that there is no single theory encompassing all aspects of human learning.

In spite of this problem the practical task of designing the learning activities and the requisite teaching strategies for a given curriculum must still be accomplished in one way or another. The most reasonable approach in facilitating this task is for us to provide a group of ideas, concepts, relationships and principles that have been found useful over the years by many educators in designing learning activities for the mature student, borrowing where we may from the field studies conducted by other practitioners.

What Learning Is

Let us start with learning as a concept. Learning is defined as a change in behaviour from one pattern to another. The change must be a consistent one, not merely a chance event (Tyler 1949). Thus, when we say that a student has learned to conduct the opening interview with a client or patient we are stating that the student, when presented with a client or patient, consistently asks a series of relevant questions in an ordered sequence and in a manner that should enable him to elicit the appropriate information with economy of effort.

What Affects Learning

If the emphasis is on changed behaviour, what produces the change? There are several factors involved. To begin with, there is the matter of the student's readiness to learn. Readiness has an intellectual component: a

Readiness to learn

medical student cannot understand the functions of the lung until he knows something about gases and how they behave. Readiness also has an emotional side: a law student can hardly begin learning how to solve legal problems presented by elderly clients until he is willing to expend the time and energy involved in working with elderly clients. Nor can he take statements from a pathological liar unless he is willing to tolerate that person's tendency. Readiness has a psychomotor component as well. In nursing or medicine, for example, taking the blood pressure as a diagnostic manoeuvre cannot be mastered until one learns the "feel" of the pulse and the manipulation of the stethoscope.

Then there is the matter of motivation. The most evident motivation of students is that they wish to practise their profession. Thus, any learning which from their vantage point seems to provide them with professional

Motivation

growth will be eagerly attempted. For example, when a nursing student is asked to assume additional responsibility on a ward he will readily accept the opportunity, provided this appears consistent with his goal of becoming a competent nursing practitioner and is not perceived as merely involving an increase in repetitious service work that could be performed as well, or better, by a technician or nursing aide. In the field of medicine this factor of professional motivation alone accounts for the altered course emphasis in certain medical schools, wherein basic and clinical sciences have been integrated in so-called body-system courses having a clinical orientation which gives additional meaning to the basic science components.

Reward and punishment form part of the motivational system for post-secondary students. Students in a medical school expect that a system of rewards and punishments appropriate to adults will be used on a day-to-day

Reward and Punishment

basis as a guide to their learning. By and large, this expectation is not met. Examinations are at best sporadic and do not provide the student with the frequent feedback that he requires. Furthermore, in his daily clinical activities the student finds that his preceptor often has little to say about the student's actual performance, other than to comment on the clinical findings. The preceptor's critique of the way the student arrived at these findings is often missing or superficial, so that the student has insufficient guidance to improve his clinical skills. The preceptor's view of the situation is that he does not have the time to watch every student perform these clinical manoeuvres. Instead, we hear "If the student observes me at work he will soon learn to do things the right way."

At ward rounds, and in the seminar room, the preceptor tends to accept the contribution of the very competent student as the standard, requiring no comment. The contribution of the less competent student may not be sought or, if volunteered, is ignored. With so many patients to be seen, or with so much material to be "covered" in the time available, faculty members feel it is not their responsibility to pander to those who cannot stand the pace. As a result, the absence of suitable rewards and punishments deprives the student of an effective motivating factor in his day-to-day learning.

Let us examine three different forms of reward and punishment used by effective preceptors. One form is direct commentary by the preceptor. A nursing student who is praised for his performance with a difficult patient will tend to use the same procedures again when faced with a similar problem. When he is reprimanded for an incomplete analysis of the patient's nursing problems, he is likely to want to change his behaviour with the next patient so as to take a more thorough approach.

Another form is a demonstration of approval, for example of a law student's contribution to the clarification of a legal point in class, by incorporating this contribution into the subsequent class discussion and building on it. The very fact that the student's input to the discussion has been used by the teacher lets the student know that his comments are valued. For the student whose contribution was not up to the expected level of commentary, the teacher should indicate to that student, in private, the ways in which his comments fall short and how he should correct his thinking to make his contribution useful.

One of the most effective rewards for medical students is to allow them to assume increasing responsibility for patients. Responsibility begins with the task of presenting patients to the clinical team and goes on to managing similar patients with progressively less supervision. Withholding responsibility from the student is seen by him as a reprimand.

By these several methods an instructor reinforces a desired change in behaviour by the student with an appropriate reward and discourages an unwanted change with appropriate punishment. This brings us to the concept of reinforcement in general.

We can reinforce learning by several methods. One method is by the system of rewards and punishments noted above. Another method is by arranging the student's activities so that, once he has acquired some informa-

Reinforcement tion or has developed a skill, he is then called upon in the immediate future to use what he has learned. Application helps the student remember what he has learned; it also reduces that effect of subsequent learning which tends to make him forget what was previously learned. Other methods of reinforcement consist of providing opportunities to repeat what has been learned in a more complex setting, or to practise an activity until it becomes an acquired skill.

Much has been written and said about the effect of practice. At first it was believed that simple repetitive activity was enough to improve learning, but studies conducted in the 1930s and 1940s demonstrated that there

Practice were other factors involved. Little improvement in learning was obtained merely by increasing the number or the duration of practice sessions. The relationship between repetition and performance was by no means direct; the crucial factor was the provision of feedback on performance to the student while he was practising. There was little likelihood of improvement in performance unless the nature of the desired improvement was made abundantly clear to the student (Lumsdaine 1962). This is the reason why it is so important for the law teacher to review and annotate the student's written brief, particularly when the student is making his early attempts at writing a brief. By this review the teacher demonstrates his expectations for written briefs and emphasizes the need for the student to keep concise, accurate notes, not only for his own use but for the use of his colleagues as well.

Another factor affecting learning is the degree of involvement on the part of the student. If he is continually observing and listening to an instructor, without ever being placed himself in the actual situation, then his

Involvement learning takes longer because it has less meaning for him. To involve the student actively in the learning is a most effective teaching strategy. For example, there is a growing trend to emphasize problem solving in current medical courses (Cutler 1985). The student is presented with limited information concerning a patient and is asked to determine what he, as a physician, should do next on the basis of the available information. He may also be given information concerning the resources available to him so that he may take these into consideration in deciding how he should proceed. By this means the student is compelled to recall knowledge or seek it out or apply it, becoming an active participant in his own teaching. For the same reason, many courses with a strong emphasis on basic medical sciences are so designed that the student begins with a clinical problem, which he finds he can bring to an adequate solution only by turning to a study of the concepts, principles, and data found in one or more of the basic medical sciences. The same courses may also conclude with sets of clinical problems which challenge the student to apply his newly acquired learning.

A special factor we wish to consider is one which for lack of a better term we may call degree of meaning. The more meaning a student can find in that which he is to learn, the less he need rely on methods of rote learning such as mnemonic devices. The key to the degree of *Degree of Meaning* meaning is association. What we perceive in new material has meaning only to the extent that we can attach the new material to those ideas, concepts and principles which are *already* familiar to us, that is, part of what is called our cognitive structure. For this reason instructors are always cautioned to provide an initial setting, or a local or immediate context, for what the students are about to learn. Many instructors provide this initial set or context by simply beginning each session with a brief description of how the day's activities are derived from the previous session. We are all familiar with the opening, "You will remember that last day we were....." Sometimes the introduction must be more precise, at other times broader in scope. The purpose is to provide an overview of where the students have been, where they are now, and where they are going. Whole sessions may be spent on this type of activity, it being particularly necessary when the course changes focus.

The final factor is utility, the use to which newly learned material is put by the students. There are two components to this learning factor. The first is frequency of use: the more often new learning is used or applied, the more *Utility* it is incorporated into the student's cognitive structure. The second component is breadth of application: the more that new learning is applied to situations of increasing breadth and depth from class to class, the more the incorporation occurs. It will be recognized that this factor and the one we have called degree of meaning are closely related.

Consideration of these principles of learning permits us to turn in the next chapter to their implications for the process of teaching.

Chapter 6

THE PROCESS OF TEACHING

Teaching is Facilitating Learning

If learning is defined as a change in behaviour then teaching is the process of inspiring, encouraging and facilitating that change. The most that any teacher can do is help the student to learn; the teacher cannot make the student learn what he does not want to learn or what he is truly incapable of learning given his current state of development. A teacher plans learning, stimulates learning, directs learning, monitors learning and evaluates learning, but the learning process itself is a student activity.

As an aside, the foregoing shows why the term "self-learning" contains a redundancy. While the alternative to teaching yourself is for some other person to teach you, what alternative is there to self-learning, since no other person can learn for you? Learning is always "self-learning", there is no other kind. What is most often meant by the term is "self-*directed* learning", wherein the student takes responsibility for both the planning and the implementation of learning activities. To be sure, a goal of professional educational programmes is to produce a graduate who will be committed to self-directed learning and capable of it, but along the way to this goal the learner often needs more than a little help from his friends, the faculty.

Faculty must be able to help students whether individually, in groups of various sizes or as a whole class. Teaching skills are thus applied to the teaching of individual students in some settings and groups of students in other settings. Conversely, the function of teaching, in the broad sense, may be performed by an individual instructor or by instructors in groups. When a teacher shares a course with one or more colleagues, this requires that he be able to work as a member of an instructional team both in planning the course and in providing instruction.

What kinds of help are needed, what kinds of facilitation? To start with, the teacher needs to prepare students for learning and this involves several steps. The first step is to ascertain what knowledge, skills, attitudes and interests, even values, the students bring to the classroom, for all of these affect the degree and rate of learning that they can accomplish. Following this diagnostic activity the teacher reflects this information back to the students, to help them plan future learning. In some cases the teacher, knowing the students' background of training and experience, then engages in detailed planning jointly with the students. In other cases, from experience of many years' planning of this kind, the teacher can present to the students objectives and activities which they will readily accept as suitable planning for their own education. The final preparatory step is getting the students started on closing the gap between stated objectives and starting baseline, by marshalling resources such as other faculty, learning materials and equipment to assist them.

Prepare students to learn

Another way of facilitating learning is for the teacher, either alone or perhaps more often with colleagues, to select the subject-matter that is to be used by the students as a basis for their learning. The term "subject-matter" is used in its broadest sense, including not only terms, concepts, principles and facts but also an awareness of conditions. An example of such awareness, in law, is a realization of the client's need to be informed of the sequence of events in a civil court proceeding; in nursing, an appreciation of how other people feel, such as how a very young patient feels when aware that a major surgical procedure is imminent; in medicine, an understanding that a patient may be "difficult", resisting investigation or treatment, because of the nature of his illness or because of some concomitant defect like deafness. All of these constitute content as we define the term in this book.

Select the content

Selection of content must deal with the surfeit of knowledge, skills, attitudes and values available to any programme in professional education. The sources of content are many: what the members of the profession see as essential content for professional development; what the public expects of the profession; what specialists in the various fields composing the profession are recommending; what task analysis shows to be essential when successful members of the profession are studied while performing their role in society; what appear to be consistent shortcomings of professionals in practice; and so on. After these sources are used as contributing information on the requisite content or subject-matter of a curriculum, individual items must finally be identified for inclusion within a curriculum that occupies a finite time in any programme.

There are three principles of inclusion that can be applied to screen content items. The first is to use as few items of content as possible to accomplish the goals or objectives of the programme. This applies the principle of parsimony; if persistently applied, it can prevent a curriculum becoming cluttered up at the design stage when certain faculty members attempt to push their own disciplines or areas of specialty into the curriculum. The second is to choose topics that are as broad as possible, so that the derivative organization of other topics under the basic few will result in a certain amount of content overlap. Thus students begin to comprehend the relatedness of content from one course or topic to another. The third principle is to select topics that are paradigms of their kind, that is, they represent classical and intellectually elegant approaches to the subject-matter.

A task that is necessary before students tackle the subject-matter is that of selecting the mode of organization of the subject-matter for pedagogical purposes. For example, in several medical schools the curricular content is *Select the mode of organization* organized around selected disordered conditions ("diseases"). This mode is made efficient by selecting those conditions which are broad enough in scope to provide moderate overlap of their content and so to permit transfer of basic learnings from one session to the next. Another mode of organization is centred about what are referred to as working problems. An example in nursing is "failure to thrive" of the young patient; in law, assault and battery; in medicine, shortness of breath. This mode is made efficient by selecting problems that allow groupings of diagnostic procedures or therapies across several problems. A third mode of organization of content is by the use of encompassing concepts that permit efficient generalization from one to another. Examples are remedies, in law; primary care, in medicine; patient advocacy, in nursing. Readers are encouraged to determine for their own school curricula other modes of organization that might be novel and appropriate for improving the efficiency of curricular offerings. This topic is closely allied to another that will be discussed in a later chapter of this book, namely curricular patterns.

Turning now to a consideration of the environment, the teacher must take into account the climate for learning in the classroom. This implies attention to both the physical and the psychological setting for learning, as *Climate for learning: physical* mentioned in Chapter 4. As far as the physical setting is concerned, the room should be as pleasant as possible, with good light, ventilation and acoustic properties and with a clear line of sight during use of audio-visual aids. Noise levels ought to be very low, and provision made for minimally adequate illumination while slides, overhead transparencies, moving pictures or videotapes are projected so that students can take notes if they wish. If students are to be engaged in small group discussion the chairs should be movable and capable of arrangement in a circle or square, so that all members of the group can view and hear each other. Laboratories equipped with microscopes should permit all students to face screens used for slide-projection without altering the seating arrangements to any degree. It should be possible to arrange, for both the shortest and the tallest student, that the eyepiece of the microscope he is using is at eye level. For problem-solving group sessions there need to be tables on which students can spread out their work materials.

Psychologically, the classroom should be a place that encourages learning, especially by permitting questioning both by students and by teachers and promoting dialogue as they find the answers to questions together. *Climate for* Much depends on the professional and personal atmos- *learning:* phere set by the teacher. He should communicate to *psychological* students by his actions that he is there in order to help them learn. He should demonstrate that mutual respect goes a long way towards developing a climate of easy give-and-take, which generates excitement about learning and about the subject-matter under study. There is no room for defensive posturing or arrogance on the part of the teacher, nor for coming to any session unprepared; similarly there is no room for total subservience on the part of the students, nor for *their* coming to any session unprepared. The teacher with the most impact is the one who is in command of his subject-matter, who knows what his goals are in teaching and who accepts that his task is to help students learn. Teachers who appreciate what students are going through while learning are in turn most appreciated by students.

Instructional Objectives

Teachers find that they must consciously use instructional objectives, not only for themselves as guides to selecting and using different teaching strategies, but also for students as guides to learning. There is little value *Shared* in keeping goals for students' learning hidden from stu- *goals of* dents, and everything to be gained by open sharing of *learning* objectives with them so as to provide direction to their learning activities. They, as consumers of instruction, have the greatest vested interest in the success of the venture and therefore are truly on the side of the teacher who cares about their learning.

Since instructional objectives define what the students are to accomplish in a course or unit, or in a single session, they also provide some guide to the selection and application of different learning strategies. For this reason it is worthwhile to mention two different classifications of objectives that curriculum developers have found useful in planning teaching activities.

The first is the *Taxonomy of educational objectives: cognitive domain* (Bloom 1956). Under the editorship of Benjamin Bloom a group of college and university examiners published, for objectives having to do with intel-

Taxonomies of objectives lectual processes, a classification system that extends along a continuum from simple knowledge such as facts and terms, through comprehension, application, analysis and synthesis, to evaluation, considered the

most complex of intellectual skills. A close reading of this system would give curriculum developers a solid guide to the development of objectives stated in a way useful in planning for teaching and testing. A summary of that classification system is shown in Appendix A. Similarly, there is a *Taxonomy of educational objectives; affective domain* (Krathwohl 1964). A parallel group of examiners developed a classification system for objectives having to do with interests, attitudes and values, a system that extends along a continuum from simple reception of an attitude or value to the ultimate internalization of a set of values that then characterizes the individual who holds those values. This second domain is fairly difficult to use and requires considerable skill and experience in developing objectives having to do with attitudes and values. Nonetheless, to gain mastery of that classification system is to provide considerable strength to the whole process of curricular design and planning for teaching. A summary of the classification system is shown in Appendix B. Workshops on the use of these two classification systems have been found essential for faculty members to become adept in writing objectives for courses and sessions.

There was also a third committee of examiners who worked in what is called the psychomotor domain; their work never came to fruition. Several attempts have been made by various authors to develop a substitute for the missing domain but no scheme has gained wide acceptance (see Harrow 1972). The psychomotor domain was expected to provide for the classification of objectives concerned with manual and technical skills.

Regarding Teaching Formats

Objectives, properly written, not only induce clarity in planning for instruction and evaluation, they also give some indication of the teaching format that may be used most effectively in helping students attain those objectives. Appendix C provides a table of types of objectives together with the preferred teaching formats. A quick perusal of the table discloses that one format can often be applied to several types of objectives. It also shows that one type of objective can be approached by several different formats, although there will generally be a preferred format because of its impact and appropriateness. Thus efficiency becomes one of the criteria to be used in selecting a format for a certain type of objective.

Statements of objectives have implications for the type of evaluation used in assessing student attainment of those objectives. That discussion is left to a later chapter.

In the last analysis it is evident that teaching is a much more complex function in professional schools than may at first be imagined. Unless a teacher takes all his ideas concerning the organization and presentation of his topics from a text or course syllabus prepared by another academic, he cannot simply walk into the classroom and teach. There are many steps involved in the working together of that instructional triumvirate: the teacher, the student and the subject-matter. See Newble and Cannon (1987).

Chapter 7

THE PROCESSES OF EVALUATION

Introduction

When we talk about processes of evaluation in the context of a curriculum we are usually thinking of two separate activities, both of which affect the curriculum. The first activity is evaluating student performance, that is, determining to what degree and in what respects the learning objectives set for the students have been attained. The various steps involved in this activity lead ultimately to the decision that each student has, or has not, become proficient enough to be regarded as having learned that which was required.

The second activity, much more global, is evaluating the curriculum. It includes making decisions on the kinds of modifications needed to improve the curriculum. These decisions must be based on information available to those undertaking the review, including information on attainment by the students of the curricular objectives. Thus evaluation of student performance lies within the evaluation of the curriculum. The latter also involves a reassessment of the setting, both institutional and social, in which the programme is carried on. It includes some appraisal of the planning process. It also brings under scrutiny the processes by which the curriculum is implemented and maintained.

Evaluation of student performance will be considered first; then, more briefly, evaluation of the curriculum.

The Evaluation of Student Performance

Purposes

The evaluation of student performance is important for several reasons. The information provided by such a process gives feedback to the student on his progress in regard to those objectives that he has attained and those in which his performance has fallen short. For the latter he can then plan remedial studies, in order to bring himself up to the required standard. The instructors, also, are provided with feedback, in that they obtain information on the degree to which the students as a group have attained the objectives of a unit of instruction, a course or the whole curriculum. Using this information the instructors can redesign the instruction to correct for evident faults in teaching or in learning.

In addition, the Faculty as an educational organization is provided with information on the individual achievement of students in each course and in the curriculum as a whole. The Faculty is thereby enabled to certify the achievement of students who have met or exceeded minimum standards of performance in the attainment of objectives and who can now be permitted to move on to the next segment of the curriculum or to graduation. Alternatively the Faculty may wish to certify that the performance of certain students has not met minimum acceptable standards, so that these students may be required either to undertake remedial studies prior to re-evaluation of their performance or to follow some other course of action determined in accordance with the regulations of the school.

The proper evaluation of student performance during, and at the end of, a programme of professional education is of interest both to the profession and to the general public who rely on the competence of graduate practitioners. It should enable the public to feel confidence in the graduates of the professional programme, just as current members of the profession should feel confident that recent graduates are worthy of joining their ranks.

Finally, evaluation of learning is the third step in the so-called cybernetic cycle of instruction. The first step of the cycle consists of determining the objectives that students are to attain. The second step is the development and selection of learning experiences for the students so that they may best attain the objectives. The third step is the development and administration of evaluation procedures in order that the degree to which the students have attained the objectives may be determined. The results of these evaluation procedures are used to modify the objectives as necessary, thereby reactivating the entire cycle.

Assessment and Evaluation

In regard to student performance two terms are often used interchangeably, namely assessment and evaluation. In this book we shall restrict the meaning of assessment to the (raw) measurement of student performance. Evaluation will be considered as including assessment but proceeding beyond it to a comparison of the performance of students with a set standard of expected performance.

Assessment of student performance involves eliciting and recording a *sample* of the student's *performance*, normally using special procedures or *devices* to obtain that sample. The sample is to be representative of the student's total expected performance. Most often the sample performance is obtained in a designated manner, such as by an examination, and at a specified time: the examination period. There are occasions, however, when it is preferable to sample the student's behavior in a natural setting, such as in a clinic or a physician's office during the conduct of professional activities. Attitudes are often measured under these conditions, since there is then little opportunity for the student to manufacture or act his response to patients and colleagues.

The record of the sample performance is taken as *evidence* of the degree of attainment by the student of some objectives set for the learning process through which he has been progressing. This evidence is now evaluated, that is, compared against some previously determined *standard* of minimally acceptable performance, preferably defined by the objectives guiding the learning process at that point, and the comparison leads to a judgment as to whether the student's performance surpasses, or falls short of, the standard that was set.

Now let us explore briefly each of the key concepts indicated by the terms *sample, performance, devices, evidence* and *standard*.

Sample

A sample of performance has two dimensions: content and time. An activity that the student is called upon to perform provides data on his performance (1) at that specific time when the activity is demanded, and (2) for that specific content (see Bloom, Hastings, & Madaus 1981; Bloom 1956; Krathwohl 1964). When a student correctly answers a test question on particular content at a specific time, it is assumed that he will perform in a similar manner if tested on related content at any subsequent time; and the examiner is conscious of this assumption. Moreover, when a student is given a score of, say, 83 per cent on an examination, this score is assumed not only to be a measure of his performance at that time, but also to be the most likely indicator of his performance at a later date if he were then given an equivalent examination. We all realize that this is just an assumption but it is made, nevertheless, in order that we can consider the sample indicative of his learning. To be sure, after the examination has been administered a student may forget items that he was able to recall during the examination, but we assume that the student can quickly relearn the items if they have been driven from memory by subsequent learning of other matters or if the learned information or skill has simply been forgotten through disuse.

Performance

The word "performance" indicates that an essential part of assessment is activity on the part of the student. The student *tests* the reflexes, *takes* a history, *interprets* laboratory results, *explains* a classification of lymphomas, *describes* the normal development of the thyroid gland, *relates* pathological changes to physical signs, *lists* the precautions to be taken in obtaining a throat swab, *detects* enlarged cervical lymph nodes, *recalls* the complications of hydramnios, *constructs* a differential diagnosis, *calculates* the water and salt requirements of a patient from given data, *applies* the principles of rehabilitation to a given patient, *selects* the most appropriate route of administration of a drug, *identifies* the greater trochanter of the femur, *evaluates* the evidence for and against radical mastectomy in the treatment of breast cancer, *summarizes* the most important data, *measures* the expansion of the chest, *extrapolates* present demographic trends to the year 2000, and *determines* from the family pedigree of a patient with a heritable disease the probability of a sibling manifesting the disease (Gronlund 1985).

All of these activities or their immediate results can be observed and therefore can be assessed directly. In other cases, particularly those involving assessment of attitudes or ethics, the matter is not so simple. Attitudes and ethics cannot be directly observed but must be inferred from the activities they are presumed to influence. In any case, the requirement that an assessment be concerned with student performance serves to emphasize the proposition that the purposes of student learning, the objectives of a curriculum or of a course, shall also be expressed in terms of student performance.

What restrictions are placed on the concept of performance? First of all, the performance must be appropriate to the objectives of the curriculum (Tyler 1949:68-81). Secondly, there is little point in assessing objectives not stated in terms of performance and particularly in trying to assess so-called intangibles which by definition cannot be used to construct assessment procedures. Thirdly, the performance will need to be displayed in an appropriate context. For example, the ability to elicit an adequate history from a difficult patient must ultimately be demonstrated on the wards or in the clinics where such patients are normally encountered. Fourthly, the performance must be at a level appropriate to the student's place in the curriculum. We expect students in their final year of medical school to solve problems of a more intricate nature, with more difficult patients, than those set for students in their first year. We do, however, expect both groups of students to exhibit the same *methods* of analysis and of synthesis in their problem-solving, the same ability to "think on one's feet", the same empathic response to patients, regardless of level. Only the complexity of the problems will change as the student progresses through the curriculum. Finally, the performance must be observable, in that it must be seen, heard, felt, or monitored electronically. Without some involvement of the observer's senses the performance will not be capable of being recorded and measured. The question of reliability of observation now arises. For example, there may be several persons observing, in which case we can strike an average in their ratings or we can ask them to train together in order to decrease variability in their observations of the same phenomena.

Devices

The next term to be explored is "devices." The devices for assessing student performance, along with their various merits and demerits, are well catalogued and described in any standard text on test construction (for example, Ebel 1979). Suffice it to note here that there is a large variety of devices available for eliciting a diversity of student performance. Use can be made of examination questions of multiple choice, short answer and essay types. The logic and scope of a student's intellectual skills in diagnosis and management can be evoked using patient-management problems. Clinical skills can be elicited by having the student conduct interviews of actual or simulated patients and carry out physical examinations of patients appropriate to their histories. The student's ability to extrapolate from given conditions or information can be tested by so-called peripatetic examinations. Oral examinations can be designed to elicit the modes of thought and of problem–solving used by students. There are many different kinds of products that students can deliver at set times, such as a term paper, a group or individual project on a given theme, or a plan of action together with its rationale. Finally, it is possible for students to present patients to their classmates or preceptors, or to conduct a seminar on a given topic, with feedback provided by the recipients.

Evidence

The nature of the evidence thus becomes vital in the evaluation of student performance. Both students and faculty should be able to feel secure in the knowledge that the evidence collected is pertinent to the objectives, un-biased by the people collecting the evidence or the mode of collection, and as direct as possible in its relationship to the behaviour being taught and evaluated. The greater the required degree of inference regarding student performance, the greater the opportunity for the influence of human bias.

Consider, for example, the situation of a clinical preceptor who wishes to evaluate the ability of his student to test the cranial nerves clinically, in order to decide whether the student requires additional practice at it or *Student* whether he can move on to something else. He presents *performance* the student with a patient, observes the student perform-*as evidence* ing the required examination, and personally checks the student's findings. For the preceptor, the student's ac-tual performance constitutes the evidence.

In contrast, consider the situation of a committee given the task of evaluating a student's total performance in an eight-week clinical clerkship block in internal medicine, for the purpose of deciding whether or not to *Primary* certify that his performance is satisfactory. The com-*evaluation* mittee *as a group* has not observed the student's total *as evidence* performance, nor even a representative sample of it. The group relies on reports from various sources, in-cluding preceptors. The evidence before the committee is no longer the student's actual performance but, instead, the recorded judgement of that performance by preceptors and others. Such evidence is wide open to the preceptors' biases, possibly in favour of the student or perhaps to his detri-ment, but seldom neutral. The problem is to reduce the probability and extent of bias to a level acceptable both to the examiners and to the student.

A similar problem arises with evaluation by written examinations when, for instance, the student is asked to write short notes or essays on selected topics, or to derive a differential diagnosis from given information, and dif-ferent questions are "marked" by different people. The person who asses-ses the student's answer to a particular question has before him the student's performance: the written answer, which he goes on to evaluate, that is, com-pare with his set standard of expected performance. In contrast, a person faced with the task of evaluating this same student's *overall* performance on a written examination does not study the student's performance, that is, his answers to all the questions, but rather considers the judgements recorded by all those who evaluated his answers to the various questions. That is to say, what that person uses as evidence is not the student's actual performance but a series of initial evaluations of that performance. There can be little doubt that this evidence is not value-free.

Further, the committee that must decide whether or not to promote a student from, say, the first year into the second year of the programme will normally consider evidence that is even less direct. Not only is the *Tertiary* evidence *not* the student's actual performance *nor* the *evaluation* primary evaluation that resulted in the mark, the grade, *as evidence* or other index for each question; nor is it even the secondary evaluation that produced the summary mark, summary grade, or other index for each separate examination. Instead, the evidence before the committee will consist of the series of tertiary evaluations that produced the summary indices for the various first-year courses. The committee is thus using evidence that consists of the evaluations (for all courses) of evaluations (for all examinations per course) of evaluations (for all questions per examination) of assessments (measurements) of performance on each question! The possibilities for introduction of bias have increased enormously.

How, then, is bias to be kept to an acceptable minimum? Possible sources of bias can be grouped into four sets: one, the statements of required performance (the "questions"); two, the measurement of performance (how *Sources* the "answers" are "scored"); three, factors that affect the *of bias* measurement; and four, the various stages in which primary assessments are cumulatively combined, as in the example above concerning student promotion.

Statements of required performance, or "questions", taken individually, must be clearly presented and unambiguous. The judge of these attributes, however, is not the instructor or the examiner or the entire teaching *Minimizing* faculty of a department or of a course, but the group of *bias* students to whom the statements are addressed. In addition, the required performances, taken collectively, should constitute a representative sample of the total from which the sample is drawn; this point has been referred to in a previous section.

The measurement of performance ("marking") is minimally biased when carried out by a properly programmed computer, which observes the responses indicated in the appropriate manner by the student and assigns previously determined scores to each indicated response; hence the value of computer-scored answers. If we have human examiners we rely on high inter-rater reliability to reduce or compensate for the individual bias that may exist in each examiner. The more the examiners are familiar with the performances required of the students being examined, and the more they give evidence of all using the same criteria in the same ways and hence arriving at the same score or perception of level of competence exhibited by the student, then the more inter-rater reliability we can ascribe to the procedure. Somewhat less reliable, though still usually acceptable, is an assessment that summarizes in some standard way the results recorded by a number of independent examiners when these results *differ* markedly one from the other.

The more widely ranging evaluations, as of a whole examination, a complete clinical rotation, a whole year's studies, can only be maximally free of bias when all measurements have been made by machine and all subsequent treatment of these results standardized. This cannot occur anywhere, particularly where clinical performance is involved, and does not always occur in the non-clinical areas either. The best that can be achieved is to arrange that the procedures be disclosed to the students at the start of the year or course concerned; and to ensure that, once the measurements of performance have been made as indicated above, every subsequent interpretation, that is, evaluation of these measurements in order to derive overall results, shall involve the same processes and decisions for all students.

To these basic ideas concerning examiner bias one further idea will be presented. At every stage, and minimally whenever an evaluation is going to constitute part of the student's official record, there has to be some **Appeal** mechanism of appeal acceptable both to faculty and to **mechanism** students. The more important the potential consequences of the evaluation, the more senior in rank or status the appeal body must be. When a medical preceptor evaluates his student's ability to test the cranial nerves clinically in order to determine the next phase of the student's learning, and the evaluation is not officially recorded, it may be sufficient for the dissatisfied student to appeal back to his preceptor. It is then only necessary that the preceptor be willing to discuss the matter with the student. However, in the case of an evaluation of the student's overall performance that may result in a denial of his promotion into the next year of studies, or may possibly require his withdrawal, the appeal body should be the highest court of appeal in the school, perhaps a standing committee on student appeals selected by the faculty council or a similar group set up on the Dean's authority. The appeal body should not contain any member of the group that made the decision against which the student has appealed. Not only should the student concerned receive a fair hearing; the whole process of appeal should be *perceived* to be fair by students and faculty alike.

Standard

The last term to be discussed is "standard." In a discussion of the concept of standards there has first to be a recognition of some form of measurement of the evidence, of reference to a scale. Such terms of measurement differ in the nature of the information they provide. The least informative is that which is limited to describing the presence or absence of certain identified behaviours. This is defined as a nominal scale (see Stevens 1974).

Nominal scale   Nominal scales are rarely used in the assessment of student performance. All that is implied by an identified difference is non-equivalence. For example, speaking of medical faculty members, if we say that Dr. A is a surgeon and Dr. B is an internist we are declaring only that they are members of different specialty groups, with no implication of rank order. In the case of students, we often assign them to teaching groups, cohorts, and the like, and for administrative convenience we label them Group A, Group B, and so on, again with no implication of rank order in aptitude or ability.

A somewhat more informative measurement determines that one student's observed behaviour is better or worse than that of another student, however "better" and "worse" are defined; this comparison uses an ordinal

Ordinal scale   scale. It will be appreciated that the question: "How much better (or worse)?" is not addressed by ordinal measurement. On this scale, students can be placed in rank order but there is no way of comparing the sizes of intervals between ranks. The performances of clinical clerks in a hospital ward are often described and compared in this way.

Still more informative is the description that provides a quantification of the difference between one student's performance and another's, in In-

Interval scale   terval scale arbitrary units. This description is said to apply an interval scale. The majority of examinations in medical schools, employing raw or adjusted scores, fall into this category.

The most informative description, however, is that in which equal intervals along the scale indicate equal differences in performance; zero has an absolute meaning (for example, the student really does not know any-

Ratio scale   thing whatsoever about the topic, not a single thing); and a measurement that is twice another measurement can be taken as demonstrating a true two-to-one ratio in performance. The measurement here applies a ratio scale. Ratio and interval scales are best understood by considering the measurement of temperature in degrees Kelvin (ratio scale) and in degrees Celsius or Fahrenheit (interval scale). Ratio scales are so rarely used in measuring student performance that examples are practically impossible to find in the literature. Nevertheless, examination scores are commonly treated as if they were on a ratio scale; that is, we calculate group means, variances, F-ratios, and so on.

When the student's performance is to be evaluated, a standard must be set. If there is to be a standard against which a student's performance is compared (and there is *always* a standard no matter who the examiner,

Same whether it is the student's colleague, the intern, the
standard faculty member; and no matter whether the examiner
for all uses an agreed, explicitly stated standard or else works
"intuitively"), that standard should be the same for all
students at the same point in their careers. It ought not to depend on the individual examiner's interpretation of the standard as he chances to confront the student. This principle may seem self-evident to the non-medical reader, but at the postgraduate level of medical specialty board examinations the principle has in the past been widely ignored. It was well recognized among trainees in the various clinical specialties that, at this level of examination, it could be more important to have learned the identity of one's examiner before the oral examination, and thereby his particular biases and concerns, than to have learned the details of those medical problems that constituted the particular concern of the specialty. Times have changed, and there are methods of challenging an unfair oral examiner. Nonetheless the attitude that was evidenced at this postgraduate level tends to carry down to the undergraduate, pre- M.D. level, for the same person who survived the postgraduate system of clinical examinations might in turn become an examiner at the undergraduate level, defending his procedures by reference to his great expertise and long experience in the field. The non-clinical examiner similarly refers to hi. scientific prestige and long experience, maintaining that he has "no trouble identifying the bluffer from the fellow who really knows his stuff", and the claim may even be valid, most of the time.

Nevertheless, a student's entire career, and the community's investment in his education, should not be dependent on essentially capricious decisions that can be neither validated nor invalidated. At least at the pre-M.D. level it should be possible for the involved faculty to arrive at some compromise that produces a generally acceptable standard, one that will permit *any* examiner familiar with the content of the examination, and applying the agreed standard, to arrive at approximately the same measure of a student's performance as any other examiner. In matters of fact there is often little difficulty in setting a standard. It is when a value judgement is involved that difficulty arises. Did the junior student extract the important information from the patient as briefly and expertly as can be expected of a junior student? Should the student have included a certain uncommon disorder in his differential diagnosis? Did an error made by the student indicate a momentary lapse or a complete lack of understanding of the situation? These and similar questions emphasize the need for a careful specification of standards, including such items as the stage in the student's career to which the standard applies, the performance expected, and the context in which the performance is to occur. The necessity of evaluation by more than one examiner is again stressed. It can also be said that the principal function of an appeal mechanism is to determine whether the same standards were applied in the same ways to the student who has appealed as to his colleagues, pointing up a further reason for proper specification of standards.

The guiding principle in determining a standard is: Is it necessary for the student to achieve this standard at this time in order to be able to undertake a subsequent part of his programme?

Faculty will define what they consider to be the minimally acceptable level of performance in terms of the measurement system used. To take a common situation, the faculty will decide what constitutes the pass mark for a given set of test items collected into an examination. If there is to be some notation of superior performance, then the faculty will define what constitutes "superior performance."

In the evaluation of student performance, regardless of whether recall of information, comprehension, application of knowledge, or complex problem-solving and technical skills, are being evaluated, each of the concepts described above will be addressed by faculty in designing and implementing evaluation programmes (Kerlinger 1973; Webb, Campbell, Schwartz & Sechrest 1966).

The Evaluation of the Curriculum

Providing Feedback

Evaluation of the curriculum can provide feedback to a number of groups interested in the professional curriculum and its welfare. Students, for instance, are concerned with it because they wish the best possible preparation to enter their profession. Instructional staff want to know the strengths and weaknesses, both particular and general, of the programme that they offer in order to keep what is good and improve what is not. The faculty require periodic reassurance that the graduates whose competence they are certifying do indeed meet the original requirements of the programme as set out in its goals and objectives. The profession desires to know the strengths and weaknesses of the programme as reflected in the quality of its graduates, the new curricular materials produced and the characteristics of the teaching staff. With this knowledge it may then be possible for the professional organizations to find ways and means of assisting those in charge of the programme to improve it and make it as relevant as possible to professional practice. Finally, the public as consumer has an interest in the provision of an educational programme of the highest calibre in order that its graduates provide a high level of professional services to the community. The needs of all of these groups demand a thorough and ongoing process of programme evaluation, which will provide the information on which those decisions aimed at modifying and improving the programme can be based.

Areas of Assessment

Assessment of the curriculum involves the development of a set of *questions* about the educational programme by those in charge of it. The answers to these questions will assist them in coming to *decisions* about the nature and scope of *improvements* to be made in the curriculum as part of the programme. Questions and answers will reflect four areas of programme assessment. One is the *context* of the programme. It includes the institutional, professional, political and economic facets of the setting in which the programme is carried on. In particular, those in charge of the programme need to know the ways in which the setting of the programme has altered over the years since it was implemented or since its last major revision. A second area of programme assessment is the *input* provided in planning the curriculum. Input includes the actual plans made, the educational philosophy of the institution, and the psychology of learning espoused by the faculty who run the programme. A third area is the *process*, the approach adopted by the institution in planning, implementing and maintaining the programme. Finally there is the *product,* the various outputs of the programme. These include the characteristics of the graduates, the learning materials developed by the instructional staff, and changes in the instructional and other abilities of the faculty who have in all probability developed particular skills and knowledge that would be of use to other instructors in similar programmes.

There are several theories of programme evaluation in existence (see Madaus et al. 1983) but the one the authors have chosen, as the most relevant from their own experience, is that of Daniel L. Stufflebeam in the reference just given. It is reflected in the concepts italicized in the preceding paragraph.

Mention has been made above of questions to be put and improvements to be decided. Questions about what? Improvements of what kind? Let us take some examples. In regard to the context of a programme, one might
Context require decisions on whether the programme is meeting current needs for professional manpower, whether the profession will be capable in the short term of absorbing more graduates of

the programme, whether the profession has redefined its expectations for graduates since the most recent curricular renovation, and whether the quality and preparation of students entering the programme are showing significant changes over the years.

In regard to input, questions might be raised concerning the plans that had been drawn up for each unit, course and year of the curriculum. Are there changes in the sequence of learning activities that would improve the *Input* curriculum and should therefore be incorporated as soon as practicable? Are there gaps and redundancies in the curriculum that should be corrected as soon as possible? Do plans exist for periodic evaluation of the degree of learning attained by the students? Do the learning activities constructed, and the evaluation procedures chosen, match the objectives of each section of the course and curriculum?

Process might be studied by asking questions about how well each instructor carried out his teaching responsibilities. How effectively did the planners of the programme communicate with those responsible for its im- *Process* plementation? To what degree was the task of implementing the programme made clear to all those involved; and what problems arose, if any, in the administration and supervision of the programme? What ad hoc changes had to be made in the programme to reduce, or remove, teaching or learning problems?

As for the products of the programme, to what extent did the graduates of the programme meet the original objectives of the programme? In what ways did they surpass, or fall short of, the original goals? What instruction- *Product* al or testing materials from the programme were sent by the faculty involved in the programme to interested instructors in other institutions? In what ways did the instructors in the programme develop new skills and knowledge as a consequence of their participating in the programme?

Basic Procedures

These questions are, of course, only examples that might be relevant to some programmes at some stage. For a specific programme, those in charge will draw up a set of questions best suited to the decisions they will face in reviewing and renovating their own programme. Then the best sources of information for providing answers to those questions have to be found. Some sources will provide quantitative answers; others will require that those reviewing the curriculum be content with qualitative answers, since meaningful numerical scales cannot be produced or defined in these cases.

The danger in programme evaluation is that of collecting data for which no use is evident, merely because those data are comparatively easy to collect. There is a parallel factor driving toward the collection of too many data: the thought that it is easier to collect all sorts of data now, rather than at some unknown future time when the need for such data may be discovered. Nonetheless, inasmuch as programme evaluation is a never ending process, it can be planned as a progressively complex task so that even the plan for programme evaluation follows a sequence and continuity of its own.

Chapter 8

THE ORGANIZATION OF PLANNING

IDEAS CONCERNING STRUCTURE AND ORGANIZATION

A Sense of Direction

Planning requires a clear sense of direction on the part of those involved in the planning process. In a new professional school almost all of the faculty are involved in educational planning; one would, therefore, expect to find a sense of direction of the educational programme widely disseminated among the faculty. Pointing the direction are those newly established institutional goals which apply to the educational programme. In like manner new goals, first put forward by those promoting major change in an existing curriculum and subsequently given official sanction, serve as guides to the planners of change.

While the direction is evident, the school must still *move* in that direction. This it cannot do until it has an organizational structure that reduces the randomness of activity and prevents faculty from dashing off in all directions at once, at the same time ensuring that nothing of importance is overlooked or neglected. It achieves these aims by placing limits on the activities allocated to each part of the structure (that is, setting specific tasks), and by making sure that every task of the organization becomes the immediate responsibility of one or another part of the structure. Thus in an educational institution there are identified parts of the organizational structure that set educational goals, priorities, and policies; that plan and operate the programme; and that review the work to date so as to ensure that the activities in which the school is engaged do, indeed, further the goals of the institution (Sisk 1977). The organizational structure also enables those providing leadership in the enterprise to monitor the activities of the different groups planning and implementing the new or modified educational programme, to sanction their work when it assists in the accomplishment of the goals and to redirect the work if review shows that it is wide of the mark.

The organizational structure must not be permitted to hamper the educational programme nor to become an end in itself. The sense of moving in one general direction has to be maintained, otherwise the interests of the organizational structure supersede the interests of the programme it was set up to serve. In addition, enthusiasm falters when difficulties are encountered, or when inspiration flags, or at any time when creative activity is replaced by routine. In these circumstances the stimulus provided by a sense of direction can be maintained effectively only when continuing active support of the educational goals of the school is shown by the highest ranks of the faculty, together with clear indications that they consider educational activities to be worth the investment of faculty effort.

Principles of Organization

From the Dean to the newest sessional lecturer, each faculty member should know how the administrative structure of the school supports him in his work. For this support to be made as evident as possible and as effective as possible the organization needs people who are trained, and preferably experienced, in the administration of human enterprises.

Whatever the structure adopted, a competent administration adheres to certain basic principles of organization. In the first place, the total organization is divided into component units, each unit having its own terms of reference which, as far as practicable, do not overlap those of any other unit. The responsibility of each unit to the others is made clear in order that the work be monitored and either sanctioned or redirected. Procedures and rules are clearly understood, applied consistently from unit to unit and generally accepted by faculty. Secondly, the organization possesses means of rewarding those who assist it in attaining institutional goals and of penalizing those who do not; and it uses them fairly. Thirdly, the organizational structure facilitates the functions of the organization; for, if it does not do so, there develops considerable pressure for the structure to be altered, and correctly so under those circumstances. Finally, a competent organization has within it a mechanism for the renewal of its own structure, whether the need for it arises as a result of internal pressures such as consistently unsatisfactory work by one or more units, or as a result of external pressures such as demands that the educational programme produce a different type of graduate.

Development of Organizations

It is not commonly recognized that organizations, like individuals, undergo development over time. Indeed, one of the major roles of leadership within an expanding organization is to move it from one stage of development to the next at an appropriate time. In a way parallel to the psychological development of the individual, the characteristics of successive stages of organizational development are cumulative, so that when the organization has reached maturity it exhibits the features of all previous stages.

The following scheme is adapted from Erikson's (1963) description of the psychosocial development of the child from infancy to adulthood. We were impressed by the parallelism between this development, as Erikson described it, and the development of organizational structures such as committees and task forces that we have observed at first hand. Closer analysis led us to construct the statements presented in Figure 1. The reader will recall that there are two senses in which an organization develops: (1) in its relationship as an entity to the external environment in which it operates, and (2) in the relationship of its parts (i.e. the individual members of the organization) to one another in the internal environment provided by the organization itself. It follows that the stages of organizational development must be defined both in terms of the organization as a whole and in terms of the individual member. The proposed scheme seems to hold whether the membership of an organization consists of individual persons or specified groups of people.

To take up an expansion of Figure 1, an organization can begin and continue its work only if there is an underlying confidence that the environment will permit the work to go forward. If this appears uncertain there *Basic trust* must be a belief that the existing environment can be improved or that possibly the activity can be transferred at some point to a more suitable environment. When basic trust is lacking, the organization will withdraw in total mistrust and avoid engaging in its defined tasks. At the personal level, each member of a working group will start contributing to group activity only when there has developed a recognition that the "atmosphere" of the group is supportive or permissive. As an illustration at the organizational level, the Curriculum Committee of a faculty is not going to engage in any reform of the curriculum unless it feels that the Dean's office and faculty in general are at least neutral and preferably are supportive of its efforts. The office of the Dean has considerable control over the environment in which a curriculum committee works, that is, over the general educational atmosphere of the school; and the signals it sends out consciously or involuntarily constitute a decisive element in the external environment of that committee.

Basic trust being established, the organization senses that it now has the freedom to go about its tasks largely independent of higher authority, its terms of reference providing not only a definition of its sphere of activity *Autonomy*   but a licence to act in that sphere as well. The members feel free to make their contribution as individuals within the organization; each feels that the organization can benefit from the special contribution he can make toward the tasks of the organization. As an illustration of this stage, the Curriculum Committee will feel it proper that it should produce position papers for study by the faculty at large, without having to make prior reference to some other superior body. Individual members can visualize themselves making independent contributions to the preparation of these papers by providing ideas for the group to work on.

Once the organization assumes autonomy it can consider taking action, expending energy in setting things going that will affect its environment. It is prepared at this stage to initiate action. Thus, the Curriculum Commit-*Initiative*   tee will begin to refer matters of common interest to other groups for their consideration, recommend to other committees that they take particular action, and attempt to alert others to common problems. The members, in their turn, will now begin to risk the expression of their ideas and to take individual action on behalf of the organization. Specific members will be recognized as individually standing for certain principles, preferring certain kinds of approaches to problems and being prepared to take consequent action.

In its work the organization now increases its proficiency and invents new and more efficient methods of achieving its goals: the stage of Industry in Figure 1. Thus the Curriculum Committee will set up an organizational *Industry*   structure of its own and delegate specific tasks to each part. Working with consultants and technical advisers it may develop protocols for course construction which, over time, will be improved as the result of experience in their application. Soon it will be publishing sets of procedures for its subgroups to follow in working with the main committee. Similarly, within the committee, certain persons will be perceived as having particular skills and talents, and the various tasks of the committee will be assigned accordingly so that the work can be done with dispatch.

In developing effective procedures the organization becomes increasingly conscious of the impact it is making on its environment and of the way those with whom it interacts perceive its functions and status. There *Identity*   is an increasing concurrence, in regard to what is expected of the organization, between those who work within it and those outside who are affected by its activities, and thus its identity becomes established. People both within and without the organization agree on the roles established for the organization and on the degree to which the organization is meeting its own goals. As an illustration, at this state other committees of the faculty will say that a particular problem should be handled by the Curriculum Committee; they expect it to consider all the issues involved and devise an acceptable answer as soon as possible. The Curriculum Committee, in turn, also sees the problem as coming within the scope of its mandate and its capabilities and will agree to work on it.

In all of this development there comes a time when the organization feels comfortable in working with other organizations on an equal footing, maintaining communication with them and fulfilling its commitments to

Intimacy   them. The members begin to think of one another as team members sharing common interests and goals, recognizing and accepting their commitments to each other in furthering the work of the group. The Curriculum Committee, for instance, feels comfortable in entering into discussions with the Budget Committee concerning its own particular needs and the rationale for fiscal support of the curriculum. It can share its concerns over the current budget; it agrees to abide by joint decisions regarding future spending. The members, as well, can put their individual interests into a general framework of priorities and live with decisions made in common. They can commit themselves to agreements on deadlines for production and on emphases in particular courses, and they can agree to back these decisions as a group after having shared their individual reservations within the confines of the group meetings.

Any organization that has reached this stage of effectiveness can now begin to think of the need to maintain and develop its achievements. Internally this requires it to train new members in its day-to-day procedures and

Generativity   in the methods it uses to modify existing policies. It must provide new members with opportunities for taking action and it has to begin transferring the reins of control to them. Externally the organization can begin to educate its environment regarding its modes of operation, its goals, and its achievements to date. This stage is of special importance internally to curriculum committees, for it is in the best interests of the school that committee membership be turning over at a deliberate pace so that old responsibilities are taken up by new people and so that the committee shall not become ingrown and self-perpetuating. To facilitate this renewal it will set up procedures for educating its new members in committee policies, procedures, and progress to date, so that these members will become effective in committee deliberations and other tasks as rapidly as possible. Externally, the Curriculum Committee will publicize its ideas and achievements widely by circulating its working papers to other schools, by discussion at conferences of various kinds and by specific publications in selected journals. By these means it can hope to build support for its achievements and perhaps stimulate other schools to try out some of its ideas or methods.

Finally, an organization will come to the realization that it has certain strengths and weaknesses in the conduct of its work, that it can and should try to improve those endeavours in which it is demonstrably weak, and that *Ego identity* its response to the terms of reference it accepted is the best it was able to offer in the circumstances. It can then live with those of its shortcomings which show no sign of disappearing, compensating for them as much as possible. Each member of the organization feels just the same way about his own part in the work of the group. There is a maturity about the organization that shows in an evident trust and harmony, within and without the organization, to the greatest degree possible given the realities of the situation. At this point the organization is fully confident and ready to expand its horizons to other areas of endeavour, for which it must start again to build trust.

When a new task is presented, the stage of development which the organization has reached in dealing with the current task may not be appropriate for the new one. People feel differently about different problems; *Different stages in different tasks* they have different perceptions of each other and of the external environment when they come to consider different tasks. Perhaps in this new case the external environment is seen as being hostile to any attempt at completing the task. For example, if a curriculum committee is given the task of developing procedures for evaluating faculty's teaching performance the organization may find itself back in the earliest stage of Basic Trust. It may then progress through the various stages as far as the stage of Initiative, at which point a third task may be presented, perhaps an "easy" one, which the organization can pick up at the stage of Industry and go straight into developing procedures for carrying it out. There may then be three tasks in which the organization is engaged, in each of which it has reached a different stage of development.

At this point an outside observer might perceive inconsistency in the activities of the organization, pushing ahead confidently on one item, going round in circles on another, bickering furiously on a third. In committee, the chairman may be puzzled when the members deal rapidly and efficiently with the early part of the agenda and then spend hours in futile, ill-tempered discussion of a later item; he has not recognized that his committee is at different stages of development in dealing with the different items on the agenda. Moreover, progress through the various stages for each separate task cannot be guaranteed, for an organization can falter at a particular stage and be unable to move beyond it without assistance.

From the foregoing it is evident that the structure of an organization is not the dominant factor in its work; rather, it is the members' perceptions of the internal and external environments of the organization that constitute the major factor.

Ideas Concerning People in Organizations

Introduction

Why concern ourselves with this topic? After all, faculty in those organizations called professional schools are *expected*, in the course of their normal academic duties, to perform their organizational tasks well, to work effectively with others and to be supportive of each other toward common goals of the organization. At some stage in their careers all faculty members organize courses, or parts of courses, or at least they are in overall charge of some teaching sessions involving faculty colleagues or graduate teaching assistants as instructors. Almost all faculty sooner or later become members of some committee, or more likely several committees, many become committee chairmen, some eventually become heads of departments and a few become deans. They carry out these and other organizational duties very well, with economy of time, the willing cooperation of colleagues and optimal results. Do they not?

Well, not always; and certainly not to the extent that there is no room for improvement. The route to improvement begins with a knowledge of current ideas about people in organizations, because some of these ideas are applicable to every level of management from the Dean's office to that of the individual instructor. At the committee level, for instance, not only does their application help the chairman make the best possible use of his committee; a knowledge of them also helps individual committee members participate in ways that are most helpful to the functioning of the committee as a whole.

Stages in Planning

In a new or changing organization the first task of a person or committee at any managerial level is planning. This begins with an examination of the current terms of reference, which have been transmitted from above, and their expansion where necessary into an agreed set of specific aims expressed in terms that will permit a later evaluation of the degree of their achievement. After this preliminary step, decisions are taken on a broad approach to achieving those aims, that is, on the design of the work that is to follow. With the design as basis the blueprint is prepared, detailing the work that is to be done. It may be prepared by the same person or committee as before, although a subsidiary level of management may be set up for the purpose. We shall assume that the latter course is being followed. The early conceptual planning is thus followed by the more mundane task of planning the detail, both to complete the planning process by drawing up the blueprint and, when the blueprint has been prepared, to put the plans (blueprint) into effect.

Organizing the Work

The process of organizing begins with dividing up the work to be done and assigning portions of it to different groups. If the groups do not exist already within the organization they must be created; that is, a subsidiary organizational structure is set up. Each group is delegated its share of the work in the form of terms of reference. Every group is now an organization in its own right and it begins its work in the usual way by expanding its terms of reference (see above). It is worth remarking that terms of reference have two components: responsibilities (or duties) and the appropriate authority to fulfil them; the two properly go together in the process of delegation. It is also worth mentioning that any group to which authority is delegated is answerable to the body from which that authority is derived, hence the desirability of identifying the source of delegated authority.

Some people in authority are willing to use the power that comes with that authority, others are not. However, the exercise of power is one of the necessities of any administration and it is normally acceptable if properly
Authority authorized. The danger lies in the use of power that is
and not authorized, or the use of authorized power in an ar-
power bitrary or otherwise improper way. The inter-relation of
power and authority is complex and often confusing, for a person may have the one without the other. To take an example of authority without power, a course chairman may have the authority to demand that his committee produce one hundred new examination questions within two weeks, but he may well lack the power of reward and punishment (and of inspiration) to enforce that deadline. As an example of power without authority, the head of a department may have the power (perhaps through control of travel funds, the allocation of teaching duties, or participation in the member's upcoming "tenure" hearing) to compel a member of his department to "volunteer" for certain activities, such as membership of a faculty committee whose decisions are of special importance to the department head; but he may lack all authority for this action. The use of unauthorized power may lead to control of another person's actions, such as

when a committee chairman finds that his department head has been made a member of the committee at a critical point in the chairman's academic career. A valuable safeguard for the ordinary member is to be able to distinguish power from authority in each case, so that he knows when power is authorized and when it is not, and when authority is properly or improperly invoked.

Power and control, even when properly authorized, must be subject to checks and balances if the system is to be perceived as fair. This implies a willingness by those in authority to take different points of view into account when coming to a decision and carrying it out. *Checks* One aspect of employing checks and balances in profes-*and* sional schools is making provision for persons who rep-*balances* resent different points of view to participate in the membership of any committee or other body charged with making decisions on matters considered to be of major importance. By this means it is most likely that the matters to be decided will be thoroughly discussed and the final decisions widely accepted. On occasion a number of faculty members will wish to make a representation on some topic, perhaps to the Curriculum Committee or to the Associate Dean, because they feel their concerns have not been recognized or adequately presented. Some mechanism should be provided for their views to be officially heard and discussed.

Once a decision on policy or principle has been reached it is not necessary, though sometimes it is tactful, that this balance be retained in the group assigned to carry out the policy, for those who favoured the decision will be more committed to implementing it than will their colleagues who opposed the decision. More to the point at this stage is that the executive group consult those interests and persons likely to be most affected by proposed activities. For example, if an interdisciplinary course is to involve members of a discipline that is not represented in the executive group running the course, a representative of the discipline should be invited to a meeting of the executive group to discuss the details.

After the work has been delegated together with the requisite authority, and attention has been given to instituting appropriate checks and balances, supervision of the work is the next step. Effective supervision begins with *Delegation* effective delegation. Successful executives avoid the temptation to hold administrative reins tightly and to insist that everything cross their desks. Instead, they are able to trust others to the point of fully delegating work to them.

It sometimes happens that the trust is only half-hearted; the responsibility is delegated but not the corresponding authority. There are only a very few subordinates who can function in such an arrangement and survive. Delegation, to work well, must normally include both responsibility and authority for action. If they cannot both be delegated by a superior to a subordinate, there is evidently a need for review of the suitability of both incumbents to their appointments. But before either person is removed from his position it is appropriate that the contribution each of them, superior and subordinate, is making to his current position be assessed by a designated person outside the line of responsibility, in consultation with those immediately concerned. Information that is both valid and reliable in regard to the performance of each incumbent will be collected and analyzed, deficiencies pointed out and discussed in private, and some plans made for supervising future work of one or both in order to assess the improvement in their work. These steps constitute a minimal remedial plan, which will require the open support of all concerned in its application. If the work improves, this will be confirmation of a correct analysis of the difficulties.

From the foregoing it will be realized that delegation and supervision go hand in hand. While delegation consists of giving to subordinates specific tasks together with the authority required to carry out those tasks, *Supervision* supervision is the task assumed by a superior in supporting and guiding subordinates in the execution of those delegated tasks. Through the co-ordination of the general effort, the sanctioning of effective work and the quiet correcting of ineffective work the supervisor prepares subordinates for greater responsibility and greater authority. In order that both subordinate and superior are seen to be on the same side in promoting effective work the superior must remember to supervise the work, not the worker. If the focus is kept on task and productivity it permits correction to be less of a personal threat to the subordinate.

In some cases, for example, that of the work of the Curriculum Committee, delegation involves setting up a subsidiary administrative structure: committees, special groups and task forces are formed, their membership *Direct* determined according to their functions and effective *access* persons selected as chairmen. In these cases it is important that the administrator who develops or inherits such a structure shall have direct access to all levels, such as by full or *ex officio* membership, so that for information about what is going on in any part of the structure he does not depend exclusively on subordinates.

The flow of information in an organization is of considerable significance and formal lines of communication must be established (Caplow 1976). Formal lines of communication are familiar items to most people. *Communication* They are implicit in most organizational charts, which show lines running vertically from superior to subordinate positions and perhaps also horizontally between subordinates having a common superior. Preferably the communication network matches the network of authority and responsibility. However, informal channels of communication that develop spontaneously are perhaps more frequently used, often connecting widely separated "horizontal" positions on the chart or linking positions that at first glance appear to be unrelated. The clues that these channels exist may lie in the wide respect accorded certain persons regardless of their official status, the special knowledge possessed by particular individuals, the continued bypassing of a block in the authorized flow of information, the apparent similarity of problems in different areas of an organization, the evident bonds created in external social activities. Other significant channels of communication form the "grapevine", a diffuse network of rumour, which has so far defied attempts at elucidation.

Poor communication is frequently given as the fundamental problem in organizations experiencing difficulties but it is better considered as only a symptom, derivative in nature, with the real problem still to be found. Often enough one discovers that important subgroups are frozen in one or another of the developmental stages cited earlier, unable to move ahead or develop. If communication channels had been kept as open as possible an alert would have been set off in the system and the trouble headed off before it became overt. One of the best devices for ensuring that this alerting system works is for administrators to make periodic visits to the sites of operation of the groups under their jurisdiction. In this way informal channels of communication are fostered.

Administrators also need to know who relies on whom, and who has access to whose mind. There are informal linkages in influence that may be surprisingly different from those identified in an organizational chart. Formal channels of communication are used primarily by the senior administrator discussing with subordinate leaders the activities in each of their areas, so that he may estimate the extent to which their perceptions match his. Agreement on goals and on means of achieving them is likely to be maintained when an effective system of communication is operating.

Formal lines of communication which follow the direction of delegation of authority through to the rank and file are said to connect "line" posi-

Line and staff tions. Each position in the line derives its authority from the position before, and part of this authority is in turn delegated to the position following. Communication flows in both directions along the line. On the other hand, "staff" positions involve functions that are consultative, advisory or service-oriented and are available to a variety of different line positions or committees in the organization. The two types of position require different styles of administration, the staff positions often necessitating that their incumbents rely on the art of persuasion and recognize the value of demonstration as role models, for people will surely imitate, given a motivation that is strong. Channels of communication between staff positions and line positions are variable from one organization to another, although each staff position ultimately draws its authority from a senior line position.

The work of any administrative structure is enhanced by the development of what have come to be known as standard operating procedures. Their purpose is to reduce to routine as much of the repetitive work as possible so that human intelligence is released for more creative activity. It has to be kept in mind, however, that these procedures are a means to an end and not an end in their own right. When procedures begin to affect productivity in a negative way it is time for them to be re-examined and suitably modified.

Standard operating procedures

Review

The preceding paragraph implies review of standard operating procedures when these are regarded as a cause of some undesirable event or as contributing to it. Reference was made earlier to supervision of the work of individuals, involving an ongoing review of this work. Review, or evaluation, is an integral part of the activities of almost all organizations and not only, nor even mainly, when a problem has appeared. The chief purpose of evaluation should be to detect at an early stage any differences that develop between planned and actual performance so that corrective measures, if considered necessary and practical, can be applied. This is too important to be done haphazardly or only after problems have developed into a crisis. Evaluation, or organizational review and renewal, is properly one of the regular planning activities of organizations, for the organizing of current work is bound to be a hit-or-miss activity unless it is based on a review of work already performed.

Purpose of review

Evaluation, at whatever level in the organization, requires the establishment of criteria of effectiveness, efficiency and acceptability. Determination of the criteria should involve those who perform the work and those who supervise it, as well as those who are to carry out the review. In some cases it may involve every supervisory level within the organization, from the bottom to the top. When agreed criteria are matched against performance, the latter being assessed through appropriate information

Need for criteria

collected through the existing communication network and by other means as required, the result is usually some degree of incongruence. As an indicator of useful approaches to reducing this incongruence the collected

Results
of
review

information is likely to identify those persons in the organization who require some modification in their assigned tasks, or who require further training, or who perhaps should have the conditions in which they work altered. In some cases the comparison of performance against criteria may call into question the adequacy of the criteria used or their acceptability. In other cases the organizational structure may be seen to require modification; but in these instances, since revisions in a structure affect all of its parts to some degree, planning for such revision must involve all levels of personnel. Ideas for structural revision are best generated by having an initial set of recommendations presented as a discussion paper for general and specific comments and criticisms. In this way each person has the opportunity and the responsibility to make his views known and an opportunity to react to the ideas of others.

Any structural revision demands the *re-education* of some or all individuals within the organization. In consequence it is necessary that retraining programmes be set up for members of the organization. Based on identified competencies and deficiencies in workers and on needed changes in organizational structure and procedures, such programmes of self-improvement are in accord with the primary task of any organization (Gardner 1965).

Leadership

In every one of the activities of an organization, leadership plays a significant part. At each level within the organization effective leadership provides a sense of direction for all subsequent levels, pointing the way for

Maintain
direction

present and future action. Part of the task of keeping a forward movement is guiding decision-making bodies so that they are productive. On the positive side, this means defining the issues and separating them from the personalities, posing alternative solutions and examining their implications, keeping discussion to the point and within the available time, and ensuring that decisions are reached when necessary. The decisions are then publicized in the proper arenas so that each person is aware of the setting in which his particular activities will take place. Not the least important feature of this communication is to indicate that the published decisions carry the authority and commitment of the administration. On the negative side, guiding decision-making bodies means preventing the resurrection of issues that have been recently decided, subduing personal animosities, and avoiding lengthy discussion of problems that are, for the moment, incapable of solution by that group.

Whatever the direction, it should be maintained by an emphasis on the use of proper procedures at all levels and by pressure for general support of the decisions reached by following these procedures.   Desired be-
Reinforce   haviours are going to be encouraged if those who prac-
proper   tise them receive recognition while those who act con-
procedures   trary to them are rebuked. Organizational activities are facilitated by those who accept committee decisions and support them, who use procedures consistent with those the organization has approved, who encourage others to present their point of view and who work within the philosophical framework of the group. Such persons should, where possible, be placed in positions of authority, made members of important committees and be considered for delegation of tasks and associated authority. The work of an organization is delayed or distorted by those who are unable to accept decisions with which they disagree and persistently act to undermine them, who pay lip service to agreed ideas but pursue their personal or factional interests as first priority, who are not willing to listen to other points of view but try to railroad their own ideas through, and who, when in senior administrative positions, do not use their proper authority to further the aims and objectives of the organization and to uphold its declared principles. Such persons should not be permitted to retain membership of important committees or positions of authority; instead, their activities should be channelled into areas with minimal influence on the direction of planning and its execution.

As the work progresses and the inevitable difficulties and disappointments occur it is a function of the leadership to encourage others to do their best, to try harder, to pick up the pieces and begin again after failure. Those
Support   who are faltering must be helped. This often involves
and   sorting out institutional goals and priorities and deter-
encourage   mining the extent to which individual or group percep-
others   tions of them are not congruent with the original intent. Such incongruities are frequently the first indication of lowered morale and therefore merit close attention so as to maintain the commitment of members to the organization.

Commitment is facilitated when a leader informs himself of individual talents and aspirations in sufficient detail to match careers to individual goals, setting himself as a model of goal-directed activity and giving credit
Maintain   to people who follow this model with the same care and
commitment   attention to detail. It is assisted when subordinates are informed of the criteria by which their work will be

evaluated, so that the insecurity that accompanies doubt concerning one's proper role is diminished. Commitment is increased when it results in appropriate satisfactions, often financial but, perhaps more often, of other kinds. Each faculty member, for example, likes to be acknowledged as an expert in his chosen field; this can be demonstrated to him in curricular matters by an offer of membership on the appropriate course committee, a request to teach in his areas of expertise or a consultation sought on the teaching in those areas. Exceptional individual effort in any endeavour deserves to be acknowledged within the group. On the other hand individual praise or blame for group activity, except for the chairman as representative of the total group, is inappropriate and potentially damaging to the individual's trust in the organization.

A significant element in maintaining this trust is the provision of acceptable procedures for dealing with grievances. With the best will in the world it is impossible to keep everyone happy all the time; some members,

Establish trust

from time to time, will develop a sense of grievance. This may require no more than ventilation before a suitable audience, perhaps the Curriculum Committee or the Associate Dean, or it may necessitate the full range of the Faculty's appeal procedures and decisions at the highest level. The faculty member has to know to which person or group he should appeal and what the procedures are for dealing with appeals. These procedures should be published and open to modification until they are generally regarded as being fair. If they are applied impartially in every case where they are invoked they will play an invaluable role in inspiring confidence in the system.

A further means of building trust in the organization is the demonstration of support for subordinates by their superior, and by each group for any one of its members, whenever this support is indicated. It becomes neces-

Support subordinates

sary from time to time that an unpleasant task be undertaken on behalf of a group by one of its members, or a controversial decision be put into effect by a subordinate who is delegated this responsibility by his superior. The general reaction to it may be of such magnitude that the faculty member concerned is unable to handle it alone, either because of the nature of the task or because of a less than tactful manner of carrying it out. At this point there is a temptation for the faculty member's superiors, or the other members of the group he represents, to lie low and, by failing to speak out in his support, let him take the brunt alone. They may even retreat in the face of opposition by suggesting that the member misunderstood his task or exceeded his authority; or even worse, by going to the length of taking counter-action without consulting their exposed colleague. The organization is better served in these circumstances if the full authority of the group is used to reinforce its decisions, either by active support of its representative or, if necessary, by replacing him with another from the group and *simultaneously confirming its original decision*. The point should be made that a properly authorized decision will be carried out, if not by a particular person then by someone else.

The leader of an organization, or of any group within it, is a symbol of its collective identity. How he is regarded in this capacity by other groups affects every member of his group, in that any honour or rebuke directed at

Show the flag

him involves them all. In this way it becomes important that he take the group seriously, continue to affirm his belief in the value of its work and his concern for its reputation, and maintain his own prerogatives and those of his group as a signal of the group's value to the organization. These symbolic activities also play a significant part in the continuing trust of members in their organization and their commitment to it.

One further aspect of leadership that will be mentioned is a sensitivity to the signals indicating a need for change. One such signal is a sudden decrease in general or specific productivity, or clear evidence that activities

Respond to signals for change

of subgroups do not seem to match their terms of reference. People tend to withdraw from the social scene and stay in their offices. Oral and written communications frequently express open cynicism. A sudden increase takes place in the number and intensity of personal conflicts identified each week by senior administrators. The level of rumour and office gossip in general keeps rising. Evidence of administrative fatigue is manifest by a tendency to avoid meetings with general faculty, an over-reaction to comment and criticism from inside and outside the organization, and long delays in decision making. These and other warning signals indicate that a special review should be set in motion, along the lines indicated above for the review process.

Leadership at the lower levels requires the understanding and support of a strong and sensitive senior administration. The administration is strong when clear and ever-present direction is evident to all. If that direction is

Show strength with sensitivity

perceived to be indeterminate or lacking in serious involvement, a sense of frustration develops, along with a broadly reduced commitment and a vulnerability of the organization to special interest groups and individuals who use power for their own ends. The likelihood of these occurring is minimized when the senior administration demonstrates its continued commitment to agreed goals. At the same time the administration shows itself to be sensitive when, while firmly maintaining direction, it allows for individual differences in perception of the goals, priorities and responsibilities of the organization. It does this by channelling particular commitments of faculty members into the kinds of activities that incorporate those commitments. The administration is sensitive also when it takes steps to contain the inevitable development of special interest groups, coalitions and cliques, with attendant skirmishes and conflicts as the organization attempts to solve problems and resolve issues. The measures then adopted by the administration may consist of reorganizing, switching personnel, or ensuring that in the membership of important decision-making bodies any strongly biased force is balanced by countervailing forces.

Conclusion

The ideas expressed above concerning people in organizations have been developed in the context of planning, organizing, reviewing and leading. Application of these ideas will help the professional school, itself an organization, to proceed as smoothly as possible with its task of developing its own curriculum.

Readers interested in a managerial approach to organizational change are referred to Dyer (1984).

The organization:		Each member:
	BASIC TRUST	
believes that the external environment is not hostile		believes that the internal environment is not hostile
	AUTONOMY	
assumes its right to act as an entity apart from its environment		assumes the right to act as a separate entity within the organization
	INITIATIVE	
is prepared to provide the impetus for action affecting the environment of the organization		is prepared to provide the impetus for action affecting the members
	INDUSTRY	
develops effective procedures for carrying out its work including the development of an organizational technology		develops effective procedures for individual tasks, trains its members to be competent, develops individual technologies if needed
	IDENTITY	
finds that its perception of its role matches the external views of its role		finds that his perception of his role matches views of his role held by other members
	INTIMACY	
works with other organizations on an equal footing, recognizing and keeping commitments to other organizations		works with other members on an equal footing, recognizing and keeping commitments to other members
	GENERATIVITY	
transmits to other organizations the ideas, procedures and achievements of this organization		transmits to new members the ideas, purposes, procedures and achievements of this organization
	EGO IDENTITY	
determines its own strengths and weaknesses without feeling threatened and uses this information as the basis for future action		determines his own strengths and weaknesses without feeling threatened and uses this information as the basis for future action

Figure 1. Stages in organizational development (after Erikson 1963)

Chapter 9

DESIGNING CURRICULA FOR PROFESSIONAL SCHOOLS

There is little problem in defining a curriculum. It is the sum of all those scheduled student activities which are planned and executed with the aim of helping the students as much as possible to learn what is required of them as detailed by the programme objectives. Institutions occasionally attempt to describe their curricula by capsule summaries or overviews; see AAMC *Curriculum Directory 1988*. For a more detailed illustration of the curriculum of a single institution, see Southern Illinois University School of Medicine 1980. But who should decide what the scheduled student activities are to be? It must be stated firmly that the responsibility for making these decisions rests with the faculty who will be implementing the plan. There may be a temptation to import ready-made plans from outside but the danger here is that no written plan can fully convey all that is expected of a curriculum. Those who implement the curriculum must understand how it got to be the way it is: what is included and why; what is excluded and why.

Deciding on Objectives of a Curriculum

Defining Curricular Purpose

In designing a curriculum the first task is to determine the purpose of that curriculum. It is requisite for a curriculum to have its purpose defined in terms that have a similar meaning for every one of the curriculum planners and in terms that will be similarly understood both by the curriculum planners and by those who will be responsible for putting the plans into effect.

This is not as simple to accomplish as may at first appear. If, for example, the prime purpose of a medical curriculum is stated to be "to produce doctors", it is probably safe to say that no two medical faculty members will agree on the precise meaning of this phrase. In practical terms they would find it difficult to agree, for example, on exactly which conditions the newly graduated doctor must be able to diagnose most but not all of the time, and what others it would be unrealistic to expect him to diagnose at this stage. Or, if the prime purpose of a law school is "to produce lawyers", what should these new lawyers know on graduation, and what knowledge is beyond reasonable expectation at this point? Or, if we are "producing nurses", what procedures in an intensive care unit should they be permitted to carry out independently as new graduates, which ones under supervision, and which not at all? These and many other related questions will be familiar to the reader who is on the faculty of a professional school, and the inadequacy of the foregoing statements of purpose will be evident.

Curricular purpose is sometimes expressed in terms of the new graduates' preparedness for further training. The curriculum is then said to aim at producing an "undifferentiated" physician or nurse or lawyer pos-

To prepare for further training sessing the necessary requirements for acceptance into an internship or residency programme, a clinical nursing affiliation, or a law firm for purposes of articling. This kind of definition does provide an indication of the *usefulness* of the course of studies, that is, preparation of students to be ready for a specific professional role on graduation. It also, however, transfers the responsibility for defining the purpose of the curriculum onto the directors of subsequent programmes, for these officials either inherit, or must themselves establish for their own programmes, a set of entrance requirements which then defines the product of the prerequisite curriculum. The problem of definition has only been transferred to other hands, not solved. Moreover if these programme directors, in turn, set one of their entrance requirements in the form "any graduate of a recognized professional school", the problem is bounced right back where it properly belongs, in the hands of the curriculum planners of the professional schools.

Similar considerations apply to stating the major purpose of the curriculum as "to provide students with the means of acquiring knowledge and skills required to pass [specified] examinations set by the national profes-

To pass external exams. sional licensing body", when these examinations form part of the pattern of licensure required to practise in that country. Aside from the intellectual dishonesty of such an approach, it cannot succeed in its intent, for two reasons. In the first place the question-banks from which these examinations are drawn are normally kept secure. As the questions are not made public the required content, depth of knowledge, intellectual skills and standards of student performance are all unknown, except in the most general way. Any attempt to define the graduating lawyer, physician or nurse on the basis of information derived from these examinations is therefore blocked at the very start. In the second place, eligibility to sit these examinations usually depends, in part, on the applicant being in possession of a professional degree from a recognized institution or having completed all the requirements for that degree. So even if the professional school tries to define its curricular purpose, or objectives, in terms of externally set licensing examinations it still finds itself faced with the task of setting criteria for the award of its own degree; which is as it should be. The definition of curricular purpose is the business of the professional school. It may indeed not be done very well, or be done badly, or perhaps not done at all, but in practice it cannot be transferred to other hands.

The examples of unacceptable curricular purpose given above are more suited to statements of the general goals of a professional school. These are *political* statements intended to enlist the sympathies of persons and groups

General goals as purposes

outside the school, specifically those who provide the money and those who provide the sanction for the school's activities. To achieve this end the statements have to be both intelligible to the non-expert and sufficiently general in nature that they accommodate the diversity of ideas to be expected in so heterogeneous a group. Declarations of intent to promote standards of excellence, to foster legal research, to provide new models of total nursing care, to produce competent physicians, and statements of similar ilk, are beyond reproach in the view of those at whom they are aimed and practically useless to everyone who has to do with planning a curriculum.

When, as usually happens, the general goals of the school constitute the only indication of curricular purpose, each stage of the planning process becomes an arbitrary exercise. The absence of overriding curricular purpose

Effects of using goals as purposes

ensures that every segment of the curriculum becomes an expression of some "local" purpose: that of an academic discipline, for example, or of personal empire-building or of somebody's hobby-horse; a purpose imposed by the group in charge of that curricular segment or by its most powerful member. How often have we heard statements such as the following:

"How can anyone practise medicine intelligently if he cannot recall from memory the Krebs cycle?"

"You can't possibly let a lawyer loose in the community these days unless he is thoroughly familiar with the details of family law."

"Every nurse that graduates must possess a detailed knowledge of, and at least ten weeks' clinical experience in applying, the principles and practices of community health nursing."

The resulting local pressure is especially evident in group decisions that must be ratified by higher authority. A curricular idea or component on which a subordinate planning group finds itself seriously divided will often, when referred to higher authority, generate there the same controversy all over again, and for the same reason: lack of clear curricular purpose. The new decision, whether for or against the original decision, will leave one or other segment of the subordinate group dissatisfied; and inevitably so, for the replacement of one essentially arbitrary decision by another is resented, even when the new decision confirms the old one. Situations like these are best avoided by providing criteria by which the appropriateness of any curricular suggestion not only *can* be measured but *must* be measured before the suggestion is either adopted or rejected; and also by which an appeal against a curricular decision must be judged.

From the foregoing it is clear that a statement of the goals of the school, however satisfactory for its proper purpose, is insufficient as a basis on which to construct a curriculum. To provide this basis a statement of curricular purposes is required, and it cannot be too strongly emphasized that the statement must be subject to a minimum of individual interpretation. It is the first duty of the Curriculum Committee of a professional programme to formulate this statement.

In the broadest sense, the intent of any educational programme is to enable the student to do things that he was completely unable to do previously, and to do more accurately or more economically, or in some other way "better", those things that previously he was able to do to some extent but not very well. As a medical example of the former, the graduating student might be expected to determine whether or not a pregnancy is at risk. As an example of the latter, he might be expected to bandage an eye correctly (rather than indifferently). Curricular purpose defines the activities, or the kinds of activities, that the graduating student is expected to perform, the circumstances under which these activities take place, the minimal degree of competence that is acceptable, and the criteria by which this minimal competence is assessed. Such detailed and well-focussed statements are often called instructional objectives.

Curricular purpose as expected competencies

In the case of a medical curriculum the competencies required of a graduating student usually include the following categories:

1. Recall. Example: Recall the contra-indications for the prescription of lithium to an elderly patient who presents with severe depression.

2. Comprehension. Example: Describe the relationship between altered structure and function in a hiatus hernia.

3. Application. Example: Provide the correct Apgar score on observation for nine newborn out of ten.

4. Analysis. Example: Determine the factors contributing to the accidental poisoning of a group of people at a company picnic.

5. Synthesis. Example: Provide for a given patient a summary derived from a history, a physical examination, and the results of requested laboratory tests.

6. Evaluation. Example: Evaluate a patient's condition correctly on examination in the Emergency Room of a hospital.

In the case of a law school curriculum, the required competencies of a graduate would include the same categories:

1. Recall. Example: State the fundamental components that must be proven in order to show negligence.

2. Comprehension. Example: State in his own words the meaning of a given statutory provision.

3. Application. Example: Determine whether a particular testamentary gift violates the modern rule against perpetuities.

4. Analysis. Example: Differentiate findings of fact from findings of law within a judgment.

5. Synthesis. Example: Plan the presentation of arguments within a legal factum so as to put forward his client's position in a given case most effectively.

6. Evaluation. Example: Identify and appraise the consequences of [a particular case in law] in terms of its economic impact on manufacturers.

These sample objectives drawn from the professions of medicine and law are arranged in accordance with a system of classification that has been adopted by many curriculum planners. There are several such classifica-

Classification of objectives

tions available to planners but the most frequently used are those created by a committee of university examiners and published as *Educational Objectives: Cognitive Domain* (Bloom 1956), and those created by another such committee and published as *Educational Objectives: Affective Domain* (Krathwohl et al. 1964). They indicate the degree to which curriculum planners must work when attempting to define curricular purposes, or objectives, which in professional schools tend to be defined in terms of professional and personal competencies.

Expanding Categories into Specifics

When general categories of required competencies, such as those listed above, are expanded into a series of specific competencies two problems arise. One problem is in delineating the degree of competence to be attained

Degrees of competence

by people at different levels of expertise. Although everyone agrees that the standards expected of the graduating student, of the specialist in training, and of the specialist in practice, are indeed different it often seems to be peculiarly difficult to formulate these differences. But it can be done, as the following two medical examples show.

(1) When faced in the hospital emergency room with an adult suffering from acute abdominal pain, the *graduating student* will determine correctly whether the patient should be admitted to hospital or allowed to go home; the mid-point *resident* in general surgery will, in addition, decide correctly whether the admitted patient needs immediate surgery; the *specialist* in general surgery will also perform the appropriate surgical procedures.

(2) The *graduating student* will recall the indications for family therapy; the mid-point psychiatric *resident* will also explain the appropriate theory of family structure; the *specialist* in psychiatry will in addition carry out family therapy when this is indicated.

These examples, culled from our clinical colleagues, illustrate some of the difficulties involved in the process. It should be mentioned parenthetically that the degree of competence defined as acceptable must take account of the methods and circumstances of assessing that competence. It is of little use requiring, for example, successful performance by the student of a technical procedure such as cisternal puncture (taking a sample of the fluid surrounding the brain) in seven out of ten infants if most students are never provided with the legitimate opportunity to perform even one cisternal puncture, while the requirement becomes quite nonsensical if the method of assessment is by written or oral examination only.

The other problem in expanding general categories of objectives into specific activities lies in the span and depth of knowledge to be required of the student at the time of graduation. It is obvious that the student should

Limits on required knowledge

be able to recall many of those facts which are immediately necessary to the performance of required activities.   For example, if he were required to demonstrate how he would quickly detect complications of a freshly broken humerus he would be expected to recall where precisely the pulse is most easily felt at the wrist and at the elbow, for without this information he would be unable to determine rapidly whether the broken bone had compromised the blood supply to the forearm and hand.

It is perhaps less obvious that if performance of a required activity depends on the acquisition, at some prior stage, of specific skills or knowledge, the latter need not necessarily be required at the time of gradua-

Stage when knowledge is required

tion. It may be considered necessary, for instance, that in order to determine whether a pregnancy is at risk the student shall have learned in detail at an earlier stage in his studies the mechanisms of skull growth. The reason for learning those mechanisms is that there are present in the skull of the unborn child certain structures (the sutures) which, serving primarily as growth mechanisms for many of the skull bones, also permit these bones to override one another temporarily when the skull is compressed during labour. This "moulding" of the foetal head can compensate, though to a limited extent, for "disproportion" when the foetal head seems to be too large to negotiate the mother's pelvis. Nevertheless it can be argued that, in the context of detecting high-risk pregnancy, the curriculum should not require the graduating student to demonstrate a detailed knowledge of the growth of the skull. Rather, it is enough for this student to recall that the sutures permit some moulding of the skull but not enough to compensate for anything more than a mild disproportion, and then only under favourable conditions. It should be pointed out, however, that there may be other and valid reasons for making detailed knowledge of skull growth a requirement at the time of graduation. If so, the case for this requirement will have to be made on grounds other than the one described above.

In summary, the specification of the degree of competence for each required activity, and the setting of acceptable limits for required knowledge at graduation, are indispensable elements of a statement of every objective (see Mager 1975). It is largely on the extent to which these two elements have been worked through that the success of a new or revised curriculum depends, for most of the prolonged and recurring curricular disputation will be found to result from neglect of these matters or from an inability to deal resolutely with them.

Professional Problems with Instructional Objectives

The definition of curricular purpose in terms of instructional objectives is perhaps the most difficult part of planning a medical curriculum. This may be because the very notion of any form of "job description" applicable to, say, a physician is repugnant to some members of the profession; or because medical practitioners are used to making clinical decisions based on necessarily incomplete evidence, relying on experience and accepted practice and perhaps intuition, and this makes it difficult for them to agree on matters involving professional judgement. Doctors notoriously differ. The same could be said for members of other professions. A further complication is inherent in the general academic situation whereby a group of experts, each a specialist in a limited area of his own discipline, must determine collectively the criteria of acceptable unspecialized performance crossing many disciplines, a situation intensified in the case of medical or nursing studies by the potentially dangerous consequences of otherwise tolerable leniency or error. The natural tendency in these circumstances is for each specialist in the group to insist on ever higher standards of competence in his own particular specialty, and therefore by extension in all specialties, creating a spiral of increasingly demanding objectives.

Screening of Objectives

By this stage, those responsible for the curriculum have at their disposal a large number of instructional objectives. These are now tested individually against the educational philosophy of the school to see whether they are

Screen 1:
Educational
philosophy
of school

all compatible with that philosophy. Incompatible objectives are discarded. For example, a medical school committed to turning out family physicians or primary care physicians is unlikely to retain an objective that stresses "the development of skills in interpreting computer-assisted tomographic scans (CATSCANS)". Nor will a law school be inclined to sustain an objective requiring of every student "an appreciation of the ways in which provincial oil and gas laws can be used to influence national energy policy". In each of these instances the objective represents an unwarranted specialization in a school committed to the production of general practitioners; and it must therefore be discarded.

Every objective developed for a curriculum is also screened through the principles of learning adopted by the faculty. For example, a proposed objective that a nursing student shall "be able to identify all volunteer agen-
Screen 2: cies resident in the community in which the school is lo-
Educational cated, and list their assets and liabilities in the provision
psychology of of health care to the general populace" will not survive
faculty in a school of nursing where faculty hold the view that
the most effective and only appropriate mode of learning is problem-solving. The memorization of such knowledge will be perceived by the faculty as silly, given that the student, when needing the information to manage a patient problem, can instantly locate it by consulting a catalogue of agencies with their terms of reference. Similarly, in a medical school where the faculty believes that student learning is best accomplished by observing and listening to faculty, and thus the first-year schedules are arranged so that each day is filled with lectures and laboratory experiments, there will be little, if any, opportunity to honour a first-year objective stressing the acquisition of interpersonal skills, such as the requirement "to develop an empathic style of communicating with patients".

The resulting set of objectives, while conglomerate, will now be consistent internally and will also be consistent with the goals of the professional programme and of the institution.

CHAINING OBJECTIVES IN REVERSE SEQUENCE

A Simple Medical Example

The requisite competencies of the graduating student having been defined, the next step is to determine the immediately preceding knowledge, skills and attitudes necessary to their achievement. For example, in the case of a requirement to demonstrate a simple technical procedure such as taking a blood sample (venepuncture), the immediately preceding abilities might be stated as: (1) preparing the patient for the procedure; (2) providing a detailed description of how the procedure should be carried out; and (3) listing those things that might go wrong and describing what should be done in every such case. However, each of these abilities in turn depends on preceding knowledge and attitudes, respectively, for example: (1) knowledge of the manifestations of anxiety and methods for its alleviation, and the willingness and ability to intervene; (2) knowledge of the common arrangements of veins at the elbow, the direction of blood flow in these veins, and the general principles of aseptic technique; and (3) knowledge of some other structures at the front of the elbow, and of the observable differences between venous and arterial bleeding. There is, in this example so far, a chain of three links: a technical skill; immediately precedent knowledge and attitude; and more remotely precedent knowledge. A few might argue that an adequate knowledge of the anatomical features requires the student to have dissected an arm, and this in turn requires the skill of dissection, which will then form a fourth and earlier link in the chain.

The example of venepuncture may be considered a trivial one but it illustrates two important points: one, that the ability to perform any required activity, even a simple technical one, can be analysed into a number of se-

Two features illustrated   quential and/or parallel component parts; and two, that these components can be derived in order of successive dependence to form a logical sequence reaching back to some elementary starting point or points.

A More Complex Example

Additional points become evident when we analyse a more complex example: the requirement to recognize when an unconscious patient, brought to a hospital emergency department by an adult relative, is suffering from, say, an overdose of insulin. This requirement demands the immediately precedent skills of (1) obtaining adequate clinical information, both from the relative by taking a history and from the patient by doing a physical examination; (2) processing this information so as to produce a differential diagnosis that will include the condition of insulin coma; (3) instituting the appropriate laboratory and other investigations, and interpreting their results. Each of these three skills in turn depends on other abilities. Taking a history, for example, depends immediately on (a) an appropriate attitude toward an anxious relative; (b) the skill of systematic inquiry; (c) the ability to recognize non-verbal cues; (d) the skill to formulate, test by appropriate questioning, and, when necessary, reformulate clinical hypotheses; (e) in the present case, a knowledge of the mechanisms that may produce coma; and (f) the ability to apply this knowledge of the mechanisms. To take just one of these items, item (e) above, knowledge of the mechanisms producing coma must include a knowledge of those mechanisms whereby an excess of insulin produces coma; and this in its turn depends on knowledge of (1) the effects of insulin and other factors on the blood glucose level and (2) the effects of low blood glucose levels on the brain's ability to maintain consciousness.

The process of derivation may be taken further but the foregoing will suffice both to reinforce the two points made above with reference to

Two additional features   venepuncture (namely, analysis into components and successive dependence) and to indicate two further considerations. The first consideration is that when a number of complex medical activities are analysed into their components some components, such as taking a history, are common to many of those activities; others, such as recalling the mechanisms that may produce coma, are common to fewer activities; and perhaps one or two at most are unique to any particular activity. That is to say, the total number of components that can be derived from a large number of medical activities is not infinite but rather is within manageable limits, *provided* one is prepared to accept that not all of the many thousands of available items of medical information constitute required knowledge for the graduating student, *and provided* the graduating student is not expected to know everything the examiners know. In consequence, as each additional complex activity is analysed, fewer and fewer new components are added to the total until the analysis of further activities is seen to be unnecessary. It is only the first few analyses that are difficult to work through, the later ones becoming increasingly easy.

The second consideration indicated by the second example is that it is possible to proceed with an analysis of complex activity into more and more orders of derivative behaviour until one arrives at something like the ability to translate alphabetical symbols for the chemical elements into natural language, or a knowledge of the varieties of motivation to action. At this stage, or more probably long before, one has to say "stop!", for the student does not begin his medical studies totally ignorant, admissions requirements being what they are.

Where To Stop

At what order of precedent behaviour is the line to be drawn which says: "Everything below this line must have been accomplished before admission to medical school"? The more useful question to consider at the moment is on what basis the decision is to be reached.

Entry requirements locally attainable

The first factor to be used in arriving at an appropriate level for admission is the level of achievement that is attainable in the local milieu prior to admission to medical school, for it is impractical to impose preconditions on the entering student that local conditions provide no opportunity to meet. The requirements for admission, then, must first be capable of achievement in the local educational system.

Alternative careers possible

A second factor to be used in arriving at an admission level is the alternative destination for those applicants who are not admitted. If the entrance requirements for medicine or law or nursing have been broad, with several alternative admission patterns, unsuccessful applicants may be able to use their existing qualifications to apply for admission either to another faculty or to a technical or other institute that has entrance requirements of a similar order and at the time has places available for them. On the other hand, if the entrance requirements have been made too specific, unsuccessful applicants will find their qualifications useless for entry into any other professional or academic field. Their higher education may then be considered, in the purely economic sense, wasted. Moreover, the unpleasant social consequences of having a significant number of the population educated to an advanced level but lacking the opportunity to employ their intellectual skills usefully are well known.

In economic terms professional schools are much more expensive, per student, than other university faculties and this raises the consideration of overall costs. An entrance requirement of, say, certain courses in psychology or physics will require additional facilities for teaching psychology or physics in secondary or post-secondary institutions. If such courses are not *Economic factors* required for admission, however, they may have to be taught in the professional school, with its higher costs, duplicating facilities largely available nearby. It will be seen that this economic consideration conflicts with the social considerations indicated in the preceding paragraph, for choosing the "low cost" psychology or physics requirement for admission will incur the penalties associated with specialized entrance requirements. An acceptable balance of these factors can best be judged in the light of local conditions.

Summary

The steps that have been described up to this point include the definition of curricular purpose in terms of required competencies of the graduating student; the screening of these objectives through the educational philosophy of the school and then the educational psychology of the faculty; the derivation, from a sufficient number of objectives, of chains of antecedent competencies; and a considered decision on the starting line of the curriculum, which comprises at its simplest the last derived link from each of the chains and which is expressed in terms of required competencies of the student entering the programme. It should be stressed that, in this way, at whatever educational level the starting line might be set, the behaviours required of the student on admission will have been derived directly by working backwards from the behaviours required of the student on graduation, that is, from the definition of curricular purpose.

The design of the curricula is continued in the next two chapters. In Chapter 10 we explore the various ways in which instructional objectives can be brought together in the name of efficient instruction. These alternative combinations must provide for:

(1) repetition of learning. The curriculum must enable the student to experience repeatedly the knowledge, skills and attitudes specified by the objectives.

(2) increasing complexity. The curriculum must enable the student to apply whatever he has learned in increasingly complex situations.

(3) correlation. The curriculum must facilitate student comprehension by scheduling related activities close together so that the learning experiences reinforce each other.

In Chapter 11 these same principles are applied to course construction.

Chapter 10

CURRICULAR PATTERNS

Why Patterns?

Objectives and their related learning experiences have to be organized in some fashion so that student learning, faculty teaching, administrative requirements and the provision of educational facilities can be effected with economy of time and effort. Patterning is the term used for the organizing of objectives and their related learning experiences into an ordered, interdependent sequence such that the structure of the curriculum, of its component courses, and of the units and individual sessions within each course, is pedagogically sound and is clear to instructors and students alike.

Whatever the content to be learned, the curriculum can be patterned in various ways while still conforming with the principles, mentioned in the previous chapter, of repetition, increasing complexity, and correlation. Patterning can be thought of as a way of packaging objectives and learning experiences so that related facts, concepts, principles, skills, even attitudes and values, are perceived by the learner as associated or related. Because of their common setting and perceived interrelationships they are easier to learn than if they had been presented as isolated components, to be learned in the only way then possible: by rote.

Patterns, then, are forms of organization, each with its distinctive characteristics, its advantages and disadvantages. Some have been historically more popular, or have been adopted more widely in professional schools; others have barely been attempted by professional schools as yet. Every pattern has a claim to consideration in curriculum development, if only to be deliberately rejected in favour of another. Each in turn can be considered as the basic pattern for a whole curriculum but, since local conditions vary and as each pattern has its particular drawbacks, most curricula of professional schools turn out to be a mix of patterns.

A Popular Pattern

It is commonly held, particularly in the sciences and in professional schools, that knowledge is essentially logical in structure, with each discipline possessing its particular logic. A discipline also has its own terms, concepts and relationships and tends to be a closed system. The *Its* *basis* subject matter of a curriculum, according to this view, is therefore to be classified and organized in accordance with the traditional disciplinary divisions of research or professional practice: for example, pharmacology and internal medicine; torts and criminal law; surgical nursing and community health nursing.

This educational philosophy is accompanied by a corresponding view of learning. The student must master the structure of each discipline and the modes of thought associated with it as a prerequisite to applying the *View of* ideas of the discipline to professional problems. Such a *learning* psychology of learning leads to learning activities *and* that emphasize understanding, explanation and description, *teaching* tion, and to a form of organization that proceeds from whole to parts, from simple to complex or from theory to practice. Reading books and articles and listening to lectures are the most common activities for students. In consequence the most frequently used instructional methods are writing and lecturing, at times with classroom discussion. The learning of associated skills is often conducted in laboratory sessions which, again, are disciplinary in organization.

As disciplines are interrelated and derivative, great emphasis is placed on prerequisite disciplines and courses. For example, in the medical curriculum pathology must be preceded by anatomy, physiology, and biochemistry, and internal medicine by pathology and pharmacology. Students are often expected to memorize much of the subject matter of the earlier, primarily theoretical, courses for use in later clinical courses "when it will make sense to them" through application. With the emphasis on course content regardless of the learner, individual interests in studies are accommodated by elective courses which capitalize on the motivation of each student within a particular discipline.

The primary advantage to the adoption of this pattern of curricular organization is that it has the weight of historical tradition and of research development behind it. Also, for many of the faculty, this is the curricular *Advantages* pattern followed during their own training in graduate school. Since the subject matter is independent of the learner, and of the teacher for that matter, its terminology and basic concepts form a common glossary for communication between theorist and practitioner, if both agree to learn them.

There are, however, disadvantages associated with a curriculum organized into separate disciplines in a professional school. Learning is compartmentalized unnecessarily. Logical sequencing may not be a major aid *Disadvantages* in memorization and comprehension if the logic is not recognized and understood by the student. The arrangement of content for professional activity is inefficient: professional problems presented by clients or patients do not, as a rule, appear as disciplinary problems in one of the basic sciences. Patients with a major problem in one clinical discipline, for example gallstones (surgery), often have other medical problems outside that discipline, perhaps anaemia (internal medicine) or vaginal discharge (gynaecology). Even so, lack of correlation of course content between basic and clinical courses is only one factor. Another is that the compartmentalization of thinking that occurs creates a tendency for the teachers in every discipline to go their own way in deriving the course content deductively.

A comparatively recent development increasingly affecting the teaching of professional course content in disciplinary packages is the tendency of research to become interdisciplinary, with the disciplinary edges blurring. Many faculty are no longer trained to be masters of a discipline; nor is it often possible. They find it increasingly difficult to accept teaching assignments in broad aspects of a discipline. In medical schools, anatomy may be used to exemplify the problem. As part of the modern trend the brain and spinal cord have been "detached" from the rest of the body, and the teaching of the anatomy of these parts handed over to a special group called neuro-anatomists, in theory members of anatomy departments but for all practical purposes members of some interdisciplinary neurosciences research group. These specialists are often unable to teach "general" anatomy to the M.D. level, nor can the generalist anatomists teach neuroanatomy to that level. What has happened with regard to the central nervous system is also happening with other systems, and in other disciplines besides anatomy. In large departments anatomists, physiologists, pathologists and others are increasingly confining their teaching to a single body-system. Faculty now claim affiliation as "pathologist" or "physiologist" only for administrative purposes and for scholarly communication, not to indicate competence in teaching a (whole) discipline. Large clinical departments are similarly affected.

In spite of these shortcomings the disciplinary curriculum is the most common one in medical schools around the world, particularly in the earlier years of medical studies. Law and nursing schools, on the other hand, have begun to take a much greater interest in the broad fields pattern described later in this chapter.

Choosing a Curricular Pattern

In addition to the disciplinary pattern described above, a number of others merit serious consideration. They will be described below. The choice of a total curricular pattern will depend on how one balances those criteria, both internal and external, which are regarded as particularly important. *Internal* criteria lie within the patterns themselves and may be identified in their advantages and disadvantages, as set out in the pattern descriptions in the next section of this chapter. *External* criteria impinge on the decision partly from within the school, partly from the institution that harbours the school, and partly from the general society within which the institution functions. These are complex matters, which we illustrate in the latter part of this chapter by the example of a new medical curriculum.

Internal Criteria: A Description of Patterns

Each pattern will be discussed under several headings. First we shall describe the structure or organization of the pattern. The influence of that structure on the design of learning activities will then be considered. This in turn will lead to an exploration of the teaching activities considered appropriate to such learning. Finally, the advantages and disadvantages of that particular pattern will be noted.

A Pattern of Separate Disciplines

This pattern has been dealt with in some detail above and will not be further discussed.

The Broad-Fields Curriculum

To reduce some of the disadvantages of the disciplinary curriculum, conventional disciplines have been articulated and correlated in order that related concepts from different disciplines may be placed together in the *Structure*   instructional programme. One example is community health science, which is itself a broad field containing elements of internal medicine, epidemiology, gerontology, paediatrics, psychology and sociology. Another medical example is the contemporary body system course, in which principles derived from individual disciplines, both preclinical and clinical, are focussed in turn on each of the body systems such as the cardiovascular system. In nursing, such courses as The Nursing Role or Medical Surgical Nursing are successful attempts to use the broad fields pattern for courses. In law, courses such as Evidence, which cuts across several of the basic (fundamental) law courses, demonstrate the possibilities in that profession. In engineering, an example of a broad-fields course is Systems and Instrumentation.

In a broad-fields curriculum emphasis is placed on the identification of themes or issues that permit exploration of each field by the students, irrespective of disciplinary boundaries. For instance a reproductive system *Learning* course in medicine might have as some of its units of instruction the problems of prolapse, abnormal genital bleeding, and infertility, which subsume areas of the disciplines of anatomy, gynaecology, physiology, and so on. The premise is that learning occurs best when all the subject matter to be learned at one time is related both logically and psychologically. That is, there is an organizational pattern that is evident to the student and that makes application of the principles and relationships to professional practice a natural extrapolation in learning. For example, to move from the normal structure and function of a body-system to clinical problems arising from abnormal structure and function of that same body-system is a natural step in the minds of medical students; the logical relationships of basic science concepts to clinical practice become clear. In a law school course on evidence, the issue that subsumes the separate disciplines (or kinds) of criminal law and civil law is the question of what the court will be permitted in a trial to take into account. Other broad concepts or unifying approaches to course content, from these or other professional curricula, will doubtless come to the reader's mind.

Instruction in a broad-fields curriculum becomes a little more difficult to design and execute. First, unifying concepts or relationships must be identified and then devices invented for combining those concepts or *Teaching* relationships as required. The most common unifying concept used in professional schools is the problem or case method, but other approaches can be used. For example, in medicine it is possible to organize a course on the urinary system around such cases as trauma to the urinary tract, infection of the tract, obstruction at various sites, selected congenital abnormalities, incontinence, haematuria, selected neoplasms, and so on. Only enough facts are introduced to allow mastery of the basic principles and relationships of the broad field. No attempt at coverage of total content is made or intended. What must be comprehended and applied by students are the principles and relationships.

There are several disadvantages to the broad-fields pattern of organization. The first is that the organization of the curriculum, and of the courses in it, requires in the mind of each of its designers not only a command of his own discipline but a very broad understanding of the essentials of other related disciplines as well. Planning is shared, so that a high degree of intellectual tolerance must be present for the concepts and relationships of other disciplines as they affect one's *own* discipline. Furthermore, since *Disadvantages* so many different conceptual approaches are being brought forward to the student at the same time in a common foreground, faculty must come to feel comfortable in teaching with others from different disciplines. There is a constant uneasiness that the topic at hand is being oversimplified, even perhaps misrepresented, by faculty members from other disciplines. This uneasiness is all too frequently evident to students in the early years of development of a broad-fields curriculum, as faculty with training in different disciplines begin, awkwardly at first, to plan and teach together as a team.

In spite of these difficulties, the broad-fields curriculum is the approach most frequently selected by those professional schools undergoing curricular revision. It has the great advantage that, in the design phase, esoteric *Advantages* topics and rarely occurring circumstances of each discipline are crowded out by more generalizable and pervasive topics and are thereby excluded for lack of instructional opportunity. The resultant course is then more appropriate to professional preparation at a generalist level. There can be no claim that logicians are trying to make philosophy majors out of law students or that biochemists are trying to turn medical students into biochemists. Instead, each traditional discipline is obliged to accommodate the others. The result is a set of courses organized in a professional pattern that assists the student in learning the subject matter by virtue of its focus.

The Problem-Oriented Curriculum

It has become increasingly apparent to some course designers that, if the broadfields curriculum has evident relevance to students, one focusing on professional *problems* would be even more sound pedagogically. If students *Structure* are thrown into the problems of an area from the first day of involvement in the curriculum, then in order to tackle these problems in a meaningful way they will want to learn the terms and facts, concepts, relationships and principles, that form the heart of the area currently under study.

Problems or cases are selected so that a defined content area will be encompassed by the learning activities required to solve all, or specific combinations of, the selected problems or cases. In medicine the curriculum *Learning* might be patterned about the problems that patients present or the problems that physicians face in practising their profession. For example, a course emphasizing ethical considerations in medical practice may include such problem areas as the mutual definition of roles, clear communication between physician and patient, the nature of the healing contract, conflict of interest in medical research, concepts of justice, professional effort and patient benefit. Similarly, in law it may be arranged about the problems that clients present or the problems that lawyers face in practising their profession.

If the learning activities in a problem-solving curriculum entail the students immersing themselves in problems and their solution, then the instructors must correspondingly refrain from engaging their own problem-solving *Teaching*   abilities and knowledge in favour of helping students improve *their* skills in defining problems, assessing problems, developing alternative solutions to identified problems, applying those tentative solutions and understanding the consequences. Teaching then becomes assisting the students to improve their own problem-solving processes, keeping them focussed on questions and issues arising from their attempts to solve problems and helping them to develop methods of evaluating their progress in problem-solving, but also helping them to recognize their own growing sophistication in handling professional demands.

The great advantage in adopting a problem-solving pattern for a curriculum is that it is immediately perceived by the students as totally relevant professionally. They can now "inhabit" the practitioner's role in a manner *Advantages*   compatible with their current level of professional understanding, and they can start to accumulate various kinds of knowledge in a useful lexicon of procedures. As their insight becomes more profound, their knowledge and the uses they make of it become more complex and at the same time more professional. Thus another benefit is that students grow into professional responsibility more clearly and consciously. This enables them to minimize the leap from performing their activities as students under close supervision to assuming a professional role as graduates.

The primary disadvantage of this pattern is that not all the subject matter in a professional curriculum is amenable to problem definition. For that reason the associated basic concepts may suffer from an *artificial* welding *Disadvantages*   to clinical or community problems that is all too evident to the students as they move through each course. It takes considerable skill in curricular design to construct a course on problems alone, and a good deal of mutual tolerance on the part of course designers regardless of disciplinary affiliation. Problem-solving curricula require a faculty that is secure in its knowledge, free of any compulsion to display that knowledge to students in order to satisfy personal or professional egos.

The reader is directed to an excellent book on problem-solving curricula (Barrows and Tamblyn 1980) in which these and related issues are described in much greater detail.

The Competency-Based Curriculum

In professional schools involved in developing problem-oriented curricula it soon occurred to faculty that if students, instead of fastening on the content to be learned through the devices of problems and cases, were to focus *Structure* on the acquisition of identified professional skills, abilities, attitudes and values, then their learning would be much more generalizable. For example, the attention formerly given to memorizing set after set of facts, and applying those facts to one situation after another, would be replaced by practice in methods of determining what information is required in any given case, seeking out this information competently and efficiently, listing in order of priority the uses to which the information should be applied, and so on. The learning, and the assessment *Learning* of that learning, by students would then be determined by statements of competencies of various kinds. Studies of the roles held by members of different professions (Flanagan 1954; Gregory 1969) have resulted, in each case, in a statement of those activities or forms of professional behaviour which can be learned, taught and assessed.

The most common illustration of this pattern is the conventional course in interviewing and counselling skills developed for students by several law schools. The total course is arranged to bring the student through a planned series of exercises that require him to build from skill to skill until he is proficient in a complex collection of skills. The exercises often involve role-playing, which is videotaped so that peers and instructors can, at convenient times, provide feedback on performance. The student displays his proficiency in these skills by demonstrating that he can interview a difficult client with multiple problems, obtain the essential information, reflect that information against statements of the law, and, in what might be termed legal counselling sessions, offer to the client some options in future actions which he then defines and describes. There are similar courses in medical and nursing schools.

Another illustration of the competency-based course of studies is the residency programme in any of the clinical medical specialties. It is assumed that the specialty has been analysed in terms of clinical performance and that the essential components have been identified, as has happened with Family Practice in Australia, with Obstetrics and Gynaecology in Canada and with Orthopaedic Surgery in the United States. Each programme is designed to require the resident to perform these component activities under supervision in as varied settings as possible, until he is declared proficient. Similarly, on occasion a physician in practice will be requested by his licensing body to undertake a programme of some months' duration in order to upgrade his clinical performance to meet set standards, which the licensing body considered were not being fully met by the practitioner. Before he is permitted to return to independent medical practice the medical unit to which he is assigned must, at the conclusion of the programme, certify that he has reached the desired level of proficiency.

The role of the teacher in a competency-based curriculum is thus to provide detailed, constructive, on-site feedback to the student regarding his performance; to demonstrate, as needed, optimal performance of the re-
Teaching   quired competencies; and to ensure that the student possesses an adequate comprehension of that basic knowledge which underpins true professional skills.

The great advantage of this pattern is that the competencies, when identified, become immediately operable as the objectives of the curriculum, with no awkwardness in translation as often occurs in going from needs to
Advantages   objectives. Needs here become defined as professional shortfalls to be made good. Furthermore, as skills are often cumulative, there is a natural sequence of objectives which permits the designers of the curriculum to build a sequence of learning activities that seems natural to the students.

A disadvantage of this pattern is that it is necessary to explore the assumed foundation of knowledge beneath each statement of competence and then to make certain that this knowledge is brought out into the open by
Disadvantages   way of *contributing* or *enabling* objectives, as they are often called. Such objectives are seldom evaluated at the end of a course because there it is assumed that the student has accomplished them on the way to attaining those objectives which are stated in terms of competencies. Another disadvantage is that it is difficult to maintain the same standard from student to student unless those involved in assessing student performance are carefully trained in this task. Only if a sensitive assessment programme runs parallel to the instructional programme from day to day will instructors know what to do in planning instruction for each session. A further disadvantage is that the programme is costly in resources such as instructional staff, facilities and teaching material. The administration of such a programme requires the greatest skill in orchestrating a complex setting, because standards of instruction, administration, and care of patients, must all be adhered to, with minimum levels of acceptable performance clearly defined. There is in addition some

suggestion that competency-based curricula, if they are to have optimal impact, require students with clear professional goals and insights.

The Student-Oriented Curriculum

The student-oriented curriculum is a variation of the competency-based curriculum, and thereby inherits its advantages and disadvantages. The

Structure   pattern is really more than the name implies, for the curriculum is not only student-centred, it is totally determined by the learning needs of each student individually.

When first introduced in a formal way it was known as individually programmed instruction (IPI, see Keller & Sherman 1974 regarding "Keller Plan"). The materials to be taught, and the anticipated modes of interaction

Teaching   of the student with the materials, were carefully
and   analysed and worked into the programme. The intent
Learning   that teaching materials and course content would be immediately responsive to the nature and rate of learning by each student was achieved by requiring the student to react to the materials presented. When printed content came to be projected onto a cathode ray tube or monitor, the provision of a keyboard enabled the student to react to, and interact with, the presented materials electronically.

We can, however, still think of a student-oriented curriculum without all the electronic paraphernalia. An illustration of the pattern is to be found in a private tutorial, which is defined by the student's goals and objectives as identified by the student with the assistance of the tutor in joint planning sessions. The more mature the student the more he is able to set the objectives by himself, plan the learning experiences, and define the assessment programme to determine whether or not he has met his own objectives. Many times, however, a student must be assisted by a faculty member in determining goals and objectives that are realistic and within his capacity to accomplish.

There have been extremely few illustrations of total programmes in tertiary education that follow this pattern, as it is so demanding of staff, facilities and equipment. Under the best of circumstances a graduate programme for a student working toward the attainment of an advanced degree would be a good example, but the pattern is more usually violated by courses offered by faculty and taken in common by groups of students, in which case the aspect of individuality is lost.

The primary advantage of this pattern is that it is, in operation, totally responsive to the needs of the student and totally determined by the in-

Advantages   dividual objectives of the student arising from the identification of his needs. Thus the learning activities, if well planned, are seen as immediately personal and relevant, providing considerable motivation for the student.

The primary disadvantage is the need for almost unlimited resources to permit the accomplishment of each student's individually determined objectives. This is simply beyond the scope of contemporary professional schools. It is possible to offer one or two truly elective experiences of this kind, but a student seeking an elective in his own or another professional school is finding increasingly that he must join a small group of elective students with a commonly held package of objectives which, in turn, is defined by the reality of multiple demands made on faculty of professional schools.

Disadvantages

Other Patterns

Other curricular patterns exist but all of them appear to be variations on those patterns noted above. It should be borne in mind that curricular patterns exist more or less independently of the various teaching methods and techniques available to instructors in professional schools. Lectures, assigned reading, small group discussion, laboratory demonstrations, continuing patient care at the bedside and in office practice, all lend themselves with varying degrees of success to each one of the curricular patterns.

External Criteria: Example of a Medical Curriculum

External criteria are illustrated more vividly in connection with a totally new curriculum than with one undergoing modification, although they operate in the latter situation as well. We have therefore chosen to present examples of these criteria by considering how they may affect the choice of curricular pattern in a new medical school.

As the curriculum is being constructed, a number of existent conditions will be found to provide both opportunities and limitations in the planning process. The stated goals of the school constitute one of the conditions, and especially those goals considered to reflect the particular educational emphasis of the school. The matter of emphasis or priority is of more than passing interest, for all professional schools have a number of goals in common, such as to improve the quality of professional service and to seek new knowledge of professional matters.

Educational Emphasis

Schools may take on different emphases, however. One medical school, for instance, may regard as its first priority the promotion of family practice as a choice of career for its graduates, while another school may regard the fostering of academic careers in the medical sciences as its particular emphasis. Although all medical schools make some reference to the desirability of improving health care, one of them may in practice be solely concerned with raising the level of medical care in its locality or within its political unit, while another may take a broader view and accept a responsibility to improve standards of health care in less fortunate countries.

When the principal goal of a medical school is the production of family physicians, curriculum planners may see an opportunity to place greater value on attitudes, interpersonal skills, and knowledge of the relationships *Results of* of environment to illness, in defining its graduating *differing* student. They may well ponder whether a competency- *emphases* oriented curricular pattern, because it is not rooted in the disciplines, is more suitable than a broad-fields or interdisciplinary pattern, and whether a clinical clerkship course consisting almost entirely of specialty rotations in tertiary-care hospitals is consistent with the stated goal. On the other hand, if particular emphasis is placed on research careers in the biomedical sciences involving interdisciplinary applied research, the graduating student may be defined in terms of his ability to detect and formulate biomedical problems, to assess critically the current state of knowledge in selected biomedical areas, and to undertake and report on limited research projects. In this context an interdisciplinary curricular pattern might be preferable to a purely disciplinary pattern.

In a different milieu, where both the point of entry of patients into the health care system and the referral mechanism are controlled by someone other than a physician, a medical school may select as its first priority the education and training of clinical specialists who will practise only on a referral basis. Here again the Curriculum Committee may see an opportunity to introduce a curricular pattern more appropriate to this purpose than the usual disciplinary or broad-fields pattern, to redefine the graduating student, and to use its first priority as a practical guideline in subsequent activities, not the least of which is providing within the educational programme the ground rules for allocation of resources such as space, instructors, support staff and funds.

Sometimes a particular goal is given similar emphasis in a number of schools and yet the connotations are quite different. The intent to foster optimal delivery of health care, for example, seems an unambiguous statement *Variants* but may conceal a decided preference for one particular *of a* method of pursuing this goal. In one school it may *single* mean intensive research into total health care systems; *emphasis* in another school, innovative programmes in continuing education; in a third, establishment of model health care units in the academic setting; in a fourth, reciprocal involvement of clinical faculty in community clinics and of community physicians in academic settings. Yet all of them are in the name of producing good physicians. It may not always be feasible or politic to be specific in print concerning the goals of a school, but those who formulate them can be expected to make their full intent known to the Curriculum Committee in one way or another.

These differing emphases and priorities should be reflected in the programme, in the dominant pattern and in other aspects of the curriculum. If, in practice, schools with different priorities are observed to offer similar curricula, this may be an indication that the stated and implicit goals of some schools are not given the attention they deserve, or perhaps that in certain schools the faculty as a group are unable to fashion an agreed-upon curriculum consistent with the major goals of the school.

Expectations of Sponsors

It is usual to expect a new professional school to demonstrate new educational ideas or improved application of current ideas. It is usual also to anticipate that this will prove more expensive than the so-called traditional curricula, if not for buildings and other capital costs then for the recurring costs of special instructional materials and the salaries of additional faculty. For this and other reasons the group or institution, whether government, university, international agency or philanthropic organization, that is sponsoring the new school will wish to be convinced that the curriculum of the new school is going to be "modern", in the sense of being adapted to the anticipated future organization of professional services in the region.

The continuing support of this group being essential, it is useful for the planners to keep in mind the limits within which the sponsors are prepared to encourage or tolerate innovation. It may be that they are seeking radical change and will encourage any and every sign of its appearance, or perhaps the group includes powerful individuals whose outlook is fundamentally conservative and who will insist that change be gradual. Some of its members may have in mind the model of a revolutionary new school in another part of their own country, while others may be expecting duplication of a respected institution in another country whose curriculum has remained largely unchanged for decades. The prevailing views of the sponsoring group will be evident in the selection of the founding dean, who will express similar views, and who can be used by the planners to test the acceptability of their ideas.

A school that is "adopted", in the sense of being assisted in its curricular planning by another professional school in the same country, or more often a different country, will be much influenced by the collective outlook and vision of the helping faculty. The latter may view the needs of the region in terms of their home country or may regard them as sufficiently different to require altogether new educational approaches.

The matter is by no means confined to what may be called educational argument, as there are implications for related matters such as hospital organization and control, in the case of medical schools; involvement in and by the community, for law schools; and the political process in nursing schools, where the profession is continually redefining itself; all of which affect the acceptability of a particular curriculum.

Attitudes of Faculty

During the period when curricular design is being determined in a new school the total number of faculty is still small. This nuclear group is concerned with decisions in all areas of the school, and in future years its members are likely to be the only faculty to have had the opportunity of achieving a comprehensive understanding of the curriculum, its purposes and ideas, and the relationship of one decision to another. If this total view is acquired, and not all of the nuclear group may acquire it, it is only acquired by having to take part in the discussions and consultations that precede decisions on every aspect of the educational component, from design of laboratory or library space to requirements for admission, from conditions of hospital affiliation to the relationship between students and faculty, from selection of curricular design to criteria for selecting new teaching faculty.

Faculty members appointed subsequently will not have had this kind of experience and then it will become the task of the nuclear faculty to provide the inspiration, the leadership and the information necessary to
Continuing maintain the direction on which they had previously
commitment agreed. The more innovative the curricular design, and
to new the greater the challenge to accepted ideas, the
curriculum more necessary this will be. Whether there is sufficient
ability of this sort in the nuclear faculty to follow through with a particular type of curriculum is a factor that the Curriculum Committee has to consider. It is only worthwhile bringing in novel instructional ideas or an unusual curricular pattern when it appears that the leadership, drive, ability, and especially the understanding, will allow acceptance by current faculty, and particularly by later faculty, a better than even chance of success.

When basic decisions on curriculum are being formed, much will depend on the educational ideas held by the faculty as it then exists and on the degree of their commitment to those ideas. Some faculty will bring with them definite ideas on how a modern professional curriculum should be fashioned, and the Dean in making his initial faculty appointments may well *Educational* have selected people on accout of their known views on *ideas* professional education and their promotion of these views elsewhere. Other faculty members, by no means necessarily the older or more senior ones, will have brought with them from their alma mater the educational ideas current there at the time of their graduation, together with the conviction that since the curriculum based on those ideas produced an excellent product (namely themselves) its underlying ideas must also be excellent and worth perpetuating in the new context. A few will be convinced that they personally succeeded not because of, but in spite of, the curriculum to which they were subjected, and they will be eager to investigate and try out other educational ideas in order that the new generation of students might be spared the sufferings of their predecessors.

It is too much to assume that every successful applicant for an academic position in a new professional school is committed to, or even fully understands, the educational ideas that are to be the foundation of its curriculum. *Primary* Just as college students quickly learn to give the "right" *motivation* answers on motivation when interviewed for admission to a professional or graduate school, so do intended faculty quickly learn to give the "right" answers on educational philosophy when interviewed for teaching appointments in a new school. The reasons why established faculty wish to transfer to a new medical, or law, or nursing, school are numerous and varied, and the desire to institute a more appropriate or innovative educational programme may not always be the most important to them. Once in the new institution some faculty will regard their current positions as temporary in the sense that at some future time, sooner rather than later, the desire for further improvement in rank or facilities or some other feature will require that they move elsewhere. Their main concern is with "mobility", that is the achievement of those performances which other preferred institutions will find attractive, whether by introduction of new clinical investigative techniques, proficiency in a subspecialty with as yet few competent practitioners, or the ability to attract significant amounts of research money. For such faculty the introduction of an atypical curriculum can, and indeed will, be seen as a threat and will then be resisted, in part because it will require them to divert additional time from their major interest but more particularly because they feel that the time and effort thus diverted will not contribute anything to the mobility they are seeking.

Other faculty will regard an innovative curriculum as a stimulus to those powers of extrapolation, intuition and practical application which have enabled them to engage successfully in their research and clinical activities, the more so if the institution they are looking to as their next home is one of the innovative schools. Their evident commitment to the school's educational ideas will be strong; the commitment of others may be less sustained. A few faculty have a natural bent toward the acquisition of power, are unsympathetic to concepts of wide consultation, non-disciplinary forms of study, majority or consensus decisions and student-directed learning, and they tend to ignore or circumvent those decisions and procedures with which they disagree. Some members of faculty like to be highly visible and will seek out the chairmanship of committees and task forces as an end in itself. Many are content to focus their attention on other than educational activities but admit to an interest in innovative curricula and a readiness to undertake whatever teaching is asked of them.

Out of all these diverse elements the Curriculum Committee must make some estimate of the acceptability of each of the different curricular patterns, so that the one finally selected might have the best chance of obtaining general acceptance.

The expression of a desire for educational improvement or of a willingness to consider unfamiliar ideas does not, however, guarantee a change in established habits of thought. There are many areas of endeavour in which

Professional v. educational

established ways of thinking are difficult to alter but perhaps none as evident as medical or legal education, where the faculty member's major pursuits contrast so strongly with his educational activities. As physician he has been trained to control the doctor-patient interaction, or as lawyer he has been trained to control the lawyer-client relationship; as educator he must *share* control with the student or lose him. As trained physician he knows what is best for the patient, his professional judgement normally above criticism by the patient; as untrained teacher he must permit the student to decide how best to learn, his teaching often assessed critically by students as well as colleagues. As lawyer he can opt out of the lifestyle he so strongly recommends to his clients; as teacher he cannot help but serve as a role model for his students. As medical researcher, whether physician or not, he closely controls the conditions of his laboratory experiments and he handpicks the graduate students who will work with him; as teacher he must work with students who are selected by others and who, although they are the "experimental animals" on whom he performs his teaching, themselves determine most of the conditions of their own learning.

It is to be expected, therefore, that most practising professionals and researchers who are involved in education will look on the strange and disturbing world of educational theories with considerable scepticism. They will require a great deal of persuasion before they are ready to examine their own and other people's ideas on teaching and learning, especially to the extent of being willing personally to apply unfamiliar ideas in the construction and operation of an entire curriculum.

In an endeavour to assist new faculty members in understanding the educational philosophy of the professional school, some faculties have developed guides to assist newer members in adapting to the structures, procedures and modes of operation of the school. As an example, the authors have just completed a fifth edition of their *Guide to the Educational Programme* for use in the Faculty of Medicine of the University of Calgary.

What is perhaps surprising is that the members of a profession as conservative as medicine should so rapidly have convinced themselves of the merits of new educational ideas that the curricula of most of the newer medical schools are based on them. One is forced to conclude that, in general, they share the frequently expressed faculty opinion that medical students will learn those things which they (the students) perceive to be important, no matter what the faculty say or teach and no matter what sort of curriculum is in operation.

This opinion, correct or not, may be the key factor in persuading some faculty members in professional schools to try out new curricular ideas, inasmuch as, although they may not be convinced of the superiority of the new ideas over the older ones, they feel that little harm *Choice of* can be done by applying them. If this should be the case *radical* when a curriculum is being newly developed or reor- *v.* ganized, then the situation is favourable for a more radi- *conservative* cal approach to curriculum planning. On the other hand, if the primacy of the disciplines is a deeply held belief, and if the necessity of didactic instruction occupying most of the curricular time is seen to be paramount, then it might be preferable to select a more conservative curricular plan. Where the decision is not obvious, much depends on the signals that come from higher authority, primarily the Dean's office. In a new school it is likely that the Dean's influence will be in the direction of innovation and experimentation. In an existing school it is more likely to be exercised on the side of caution.

Faculty Organization

It is helpful when the Faculty organization and the curricular design complement one another. In matters of organization the Dean may possess powers of final decision on specific matters affecting his Faculty, yet the consultative procedures leading up to these decisions, and thus the structure of the Faculty, may take many different forms.

Faculties of Medicine, for example, have historically been hierarchical and in many of the modern schools this is still the case. In the hierarchical form of organization, recommendations originating or approved at

*Types
of
organization*
one level must be passed for consideration to the next higher level and may there be approved, modified, reversed, suppressed or referred back. An essential feature is that progressively higher levels of authority involve progressively more senior ranking faculty, so that the recommendations and advice that the Dean officially receives are channelled exclusively through department heads or their equivalents. Decisions, once taken, are in turn communicated down the hierarchy to the working levels. At the opposite extreme of organization is the unstructured system in which the Dean selects individuals, or appoints ad hoc committees, to investigate and advise on specific matters and report directly to him. His decisions are addressed to selected audiences, not necessarily the whole Faculty. An intermediate position might consist of a democratic type of organization in which committee membership is independent of academic rank and achieved through Faculty-wide elections, and in which opinions and recommendations are sought from all appropriate committees and then from the Faculty Council. Decisions in turn are communicated back to the Faculty Council. Many will recognize this form as being most appropriate to contemporary academic values. Law and nursing faculties are often organized in this way.

By whatever methods the Dean receives suggestions, recommendations, opinions and advice from the faculty-at-large there remains the question of whether he considers recommendations to be purely advisory, as perhaps they must often be in the strictly formal sense, or whether he regards them as binding in practical terms, provided they do not contravene the by-laws or policies of the parent institution. It takes a courageous dean, or a very astute dean, to assume this latter position, for it will occasionally put him in the situation of having to promote or defend some measure to which he is seemingly opposed.

Similar considerations apply to the head of each administrative unit of the Faculty. These units may be constituted in various ways. The most frequent arrangement is by discipline, the administrative unit being then con-

*Administrative
units*
cerned with a single discipline, for example the Department of Psychiatry, or occasionally a group of disciplines, for example the Department of Basic Medical Sciences. The department deals with all aspects of the disci̯line(s)

concerned: education (medical, paramedical, non-medical), research, graduate studies, service activities, faculty development, recommendations for appointment and promotion of its members, and so on. The other primary administrative arrangement is by function rather than by discipline, so that each function (research, professional service, education, administration) has its own administrative unit and the faculty member is part of as many units as he has academic functions. Whatever the administrative unit, it may be organized internally as a hierarchy, an unstructured system or some form of democratic system.

Organizations, once set up and functioning, are difficult to change except in minor ways, barring an outright revolt. The organization sets constraints on the curricular patterns that can be initiated and maintained. A
Relation to faculty group wishing to effect a change from a totally
curricular student-oriented curricular pattern to a disciplinary pat-
pattern tern might find one of its major tasks to be persuading
faculty who have become accustomed to a functional type of Faculty organization to accept a disciplinary mode of organization. In a new school the design of the curriculum is usually determined at an early enough stage that the mode of Faculty organization has not been formalized or can still be redirected. If that is the case, the choice of curricular design need not be influenced by existing organizational structure, provided there is no strong pressure from the parent institution or the sponsors to conform to some given type. With the freedom to shape both the curriculum and the Faculty organization the planners need only seek to make them compatible. A nondisciplinary curricular pattern might only be possible in a nondisciplinary Faculty organization. A broad-fields pattern might work well with either a functional or a disciplinary organization, but a problem-oriented pattern could be incompatible with a hierarchical form of departmental structure.

Licensing Requirements

A professional curriculum will also be influenced by the requirements for licensing. For example, in order to practise medicine a physician must be licensed by a local or national licensing body. The educational requirements for licensing may be limited to proof that a medical degree has been obtained from an approved medical school; they may also require the applicant to have passed an examination set by, or under the auspices of, the licensing body; and they may further require the applicant to have undertaken specified educational and clinical activities. Each of these requirements will be considered in turn as it relates to the medical school curriculum.

The first requirement is a medical degree obtained from an approved medical school. This gives to the medical school absolute control over its curriculum, subject only to the conditions that have to be met in order that

A professional degree

government and institutional approval be initially granted and periodically renewed. These conditions are mostly concerned with the adequacy of facilities and staffing and to a much lesser extent with the details of curriculum. They do not, therefore, affect significantly the curricular patterns adopted by the school.

The second requirement for licensing, involving a special examination, provides at the same time a challenge to the curriculum and a psychological impediment to it. The challenge is that graduates of a new or radically

A special examination

revised curriculum are expected to perform as well as, or better than, their contemporaries from other medical schools in licensing examinations. On the other hand, the current and the new curricula may well have differing emphases. The one may emphasize recall of specific data, the other stressing critical appraisal of data; one may be concerned more with disease-entities, the other with disease-processes; one may concentrate on the individual unhealthy patient, the other on the unhealthy community; the one concerned more with curative treatment, the other with various levels of prevention. Despite this, an external examination required by a licensing body, particularly at the national level, is most likely to reflect the emphases of the faculties in the majority of existing medical schools and so contain an intrinsic bias favouring students from the older schools with their traditional types of curriculum.

Any professional school with an innovative curriculum may then find its graduates compared unfavourably with those of traditional schools on the basis of group performance in these examinations, and its faculty may be discouraged by

Bias in the examination

this result. The situation is analogous to the application of the same intelligence test to people from two cultures, the candidates from one culture doing better than those from the other culture for the reason that the test was constructed by members of the former group. It is not that one group is more intelligent than the other but that the groups place their emphases on different activities, and no single test is equally fair to both groups. In the case of an external examination for medical licensure, the graduating class of an innovative or unusual curriculum should no more be condemned for performance below the national mean than congratulated for performance above the national mean, for in either case comparisons are simply not valid. Consistent group performance above the national mean over a period of years may in fact raise doubts about the innovativeness of a "new" curriculum in practice and perhaps ought to stimulate an internal inquiry into the relationship of declared educational aims and methods to actual activities of student learning and faculty teaching.

It is the third requirement for licensing, having to do with specific educational activities, that most affects curricular planning. The more specific and the more numerous these mandatory activities, the less oppor-

Specified activities tunity may be afforded for curricular innovation. For example, a licensing requirement that the medical applicant shall have taken courses in medical biochemistry and human pathology consisting of at least one hundred hours each of lectures and laboratory work per course would, on the surface, rule out all curricular patterns other than the disciplinary one. Similarly, a clinical requirement for block periods of time spent clerking on specific kinds of wards in teaching hospitals (such as minimally eight weeks each on wards allocated to the major specialties: internal medicine, surgery, paediatrics, etc.) would again severely restrict the choice of curricular pattern by making the practicalities of most options unduly difficult. If such were the case, a problem-oriented or competency-oriented pattern would require the problems or competencies to be sorted out into sets labelled "medical," "surgical," "paediatric," and so on, and these in turn into "clinical" and "non-clinical," in order to be compatible with the licensing requirements. A broad-fields interdisciplinary pattern would be impossible to reconcile with the disciplinary hospital ward organization that must exist if these licensing requirements are to be capable of fulfilment. Licensing regulations are the most important external factor in curricular design, for their neglect may result in the production of physicians who will not be licensed to practise medicine.

Access to Patients

In the design of a professional curriculum the matter of access to patients or clients is a crucial consideration. Access is required for practice in techniques of clinical examination, especially interviewing, in a context provid-

Benefits of access ing unique motivation which no technological gadgetry or simulation can replace. It is required also to provide opportunities for the student to seek out and recognize in sick people those physical signs which are not present in the person who is well. A clinical setting provides the best or the only means whereby the medical or nursing student can acquire professional attitudes toward patients and can begin to comprehend the interaction of person and environment that produces illness. It is the only means by which the student can understand the reaction of the patient to his illness, the impact of chronic illness or disability on a patient's daily life and personal relationships, and the degree to which a patient's attitudes affect those measures of prevention, treatment and rehabilitation intended for his benefit. Not least, a clinical setting provides opportunities for the student to assume increasing degrees of responsibility, under supervision, for the care of patients. A similar argument can be made for clinical experiences for law students in the later years of their professional programme.

Until recently the emphasis in medicine and nursing has been almost exclusively on access to patients occupying beds in what are referred to as teaching hospitals, especially those hospitals providing tertiary care. The *Teaching hospitals* advantages of using mainly hospital patients are many. In a teaching hospital there are large numbers of patients conveniently located in one area, the patients collectively display evidence of a great variety of different diseases including some of the rare ones, many highly qualified medical and nursing specialists are available as teachers and there are extensive ancillary facilities. An emergency department is usually present and in some hospitals there are active outpatient clinics. Faculty believe that teaching hospitals demand a high level of medical and nursing care, so that students see "good medicine". It is difficult to think of a medical or a nursing school functioning well without access to patients in one or more hospitals; and, indeed, in some countries a school will not be accredited unless there is available, on the average per student, some minimal number of beds in teaching hospitals.

Hospital experience alone may perhaps be considered to provide sufficient access to patients when the expected behaviours of the graduating medical student are defined within the context of hospital practice, whether *Focus on in-hospital practice* this context is stated or implied. In many instances the fact that each and every new graduate proceeds into a hospital-based internship or residency reinforces this context, for then the medical student tends to see his studies as a preparation for the immediate hospital-based programme rather than for the later independent practice of medicine. Faculty instructors are tempted to encourage this outlook, for their personal workload in the care of hospital patients is made lighter when the intern or resident is familiar with the routines, organization and problems of hospital practice and is not distracted by matters which, valuable though they may be in other circumstances, are at best irrelevant to the practice of in-hospital medicine.

The many advantages of using hospitals as the sole or principal source of patients, particularly from the faculty's point of view, have in the past far outweighed the disadvantages. These disadvantages include the sig- *Disadvantages* nificant fact that the teaching hospital experience is far different from the type of practice in which most students will engage when their training is complete. For many, their ability at that time to provide tertiary care in expensively equipped teaching centres will be quite simply irrelevant. In addition, even in those hospitals which have outpatient clinics the student has little or no opportunity to undertake the tasks that will occupy much of his time in his own future practice, for example managing in their own environment those sick patients who need not be admitted to hospital and those who have been discharged from hospital; instituting and supervising preventive measures; educating patients and their families to participate in the maintenance or restoration of their normal functioning; deciding whether or not to admit patients to the hospital; performing minor surgery; and selecting and supervising appropriate forms of nonphysician assistance in treatment, rehabilitation and daily living.

As a result of these considerations the provision of access to patients in teaching hospitals, while necessary, is no longer considered sufficient. For some medical schools they are not even considered necessary. These *Community hospitals* schools prefer to provide clinical instruction in community hospitals affiliated with, rather than owned or controlled by, the medical school, feeling that students will benefit pedagogically from the broad spectrum of patients available in them. If the hospitals are functioning effectively they will include patients involved in primary, secondary and tertiary care.

The development of medical and nursing skills relating to the patient in his total environment, and not only the in-hospital part of it, requires access to patients in other than hospital contexts. The usual sources may *Non-hospital contexts* include physicians' offices, local medical clinics and patients' homes. Should some of these sources not yet be available, their development would be a matter for immediate administrative attention so that they will be available when they are first needed. It is likely that in a new school some preliminary inquiries in this direction will have been made before the decision was taken to develop the school, and the information so obtained will determine whether or not progress along these lines is possible or likely. The design of the curriculum, and the curricular patterns chosen, will be markedly influenced by the availability of these sources of patients for teaching. The North American experience over the past twenty years with using physicians in outlying areas as volunteer preceptors has been most positive. The response by these physicians to requests that they serve in such a capacity has been strong, and in general those physicians have been equally forthright in sharing the idiosyncrasies of their individual practices with students. Students have in turn responded with hard work and strong professional commitment. Both student and preceptor have benefitted.

However, it is not only, or in some regions not even principally, with the individual patient that the physician or nurse is concerned, nor exclusively with the individual who is ill. The concern may also be with the

Varieties of   family as "patient," with special groups in the popula-
"patient"   tion who are in some particular respect at risk, with the
community as an entity, and with groups of the disabled who can benefit significantly from forms of management involving other health personnel and volunteer helpers. In order to become aware of such problems the student needs access to various kinds of health-care agencies such as family counselling units, well-baby clinics, drug crisis centres, public health departments and their numerous offshoots, home-care agencies, and some of the voluntary health organizations. When these various facilities are available it is possible to institute a programme that is not so highly dependent on the hospitals, whether this is desirable per se or whether the hospitals alone cannot provide enough patients or enough of a variety of problems for teaching purposes. Should these health-care facilities not be available, or their co-operation with the school for any reason unlikely to be forthcoming in the reasonable future, liaison with the local hospitals assumes greater importance and the choice of curricular pattern is significantly restricted.

Summary

The internal criteria governing the choice of a curricular pattern include a compatibility between the capabilities of the students, the capabilities of the faculty, the objectives of the curriculum and the resources realistically available to students and teachers in planning and realizing the learning activities. The external criteria, in the example given of a medical school curriculum, include the goals of the school, the attitudes and motivations of the faculty, the Faculty organization, licensing requirements and access to patients. In the course of the above discussion it will have become obvious that the choice of a particular pattern, for good and sufficient reasons, has a definite impact on the structure of the courses that are designed within that curriculum. It is to course design that we now turn our attention in the next few chapters.

Chapter 11

COURSE DESIGN

Introduction

Course design as a process is largely derivative in nature, the decisions made during this process relying on principles and procedures found primarily in Chapter 5 on learning and in Chapter 6 on teaching. The reader may find it helpful to review the content of those chapters before proceeding.

The design of courses begins from the assembled instructional objectives determined as described in Chapter 9. The steps to be taken are summarized as follows. The objectives are organized into a number of sets, each set of objectives forming the basis of one course. The common themes of these courses are identified. An order of presentation of courses is then determined. The principle underlying this particular progression of courses is identified.

For each course a period of time is allocated within which most students are expected to complete it. The objectives for any course may in turn be divided into a number of subsets, each subset forming the basis of a separate unit of instruction within the course. An order of presentation of these units is also determined. For u nits, as well as for courses, an element of continuity and a principle of progression are identified. Finally, teaching sessions are set up, directed toward student achievement of unit or course objectives and using methods of teaching and learning appropriate to the nature of each objective to be achieved.

These various steps will now be described more fully.

Determination of Courses

Starting with Chained Objectives

By the stage reached at the end of Chapter 9 those responsible for the curriculum have at their disposal a large number of instructional objectives, appropriately screened. The objectives are not arranged randomly for, as described in Chapter 9, most of them are *derived* from a much smaller original set that constitutes the definition of the graduating student. The process of derivation is usually based on dependence, that is, by determining which ones are prerequisite to others and it may be pointed out that there are various systems of dependence from which to choose. For example, one sequence of objectives may be built on prerequisite skills, another on prerequisite knowledge, and a third on a combination of these two.

The total objectives, then, are already arranged as a number of *chains*, each chain starting from a single "graduation" objective and leading backwards, so to speak, via numerous intermediate links to one or more of the "admission" objectives at the arbitrarily defined cutoff line. This is the simplest case, and we do not mean to imply that every single chain reaches back to an "admission" objective, nor to deny that chains may branch or converge or interconnect. However, each *must* link to a "graduation" objective either directly or via another chain and, if any one of them does not do so, its right to survive must be openly challenged.

A further consideration in chaining is that the way in which objectives are stated and dependent objectives are derived is apt to be bound up with a particular view of teaching and learning. The "what" and the "how" of curricular planning are not, in practice, totally independent of one another. Those who believe in the disciplines, for instance, as the basis for teaching and learning will tend to formulate objectives in disciplinary terms and to derive dependent objectives in a similar way, with a view to developing a disciplinary type of curriculum. Those who favour the use of competencies rather than disciplines will be more likely to express and derive objectives in terms of competencies, with a view to developing a competency-based curriculum. The topic of types of curriculum, or curricular patterns, has been dealt with in some detail in Chapter 10, and it will suffice here to state that a preference for a particular curricular pattern both influences, and is influenced by, the manner in which objectives are stated and derived.

Identifying Courses

The way in which the objectives have been chained also supplies the framework for deciding how the total number of objectives shall be subdivided into manageable portions. These portions will here be called courses, although the reader may substitute some preferred term such as phases or themes. In the most general terms a single chain of objectives may form the basis for a whole course, a part of a course, or more than one

Defining
a
course

course. When chains converge or branch, the way is open for individual initiative in creating new and more effective assemblages of objectives as courses. A course is thus defined by the set of objectives chosen to serve as the purposes of that course.

It can be assumed that those who assemble the objectives into packages (courses) have some guiding concept or theme, stated or unstated, that they

Continuity
between
courses

consistently use in so doing. Whatever it is, it constitutes their view of the element of continuity that runs through all the courses and so, as an aid to comprehension of the curriculum, it deserves to be made known to faculty and students alike as the organizing element of the curriculum.

One factor having a major influence in delimiting courses is that of time, or the expected duration of courses. It is usual to think of a curriculum as consisting of a number of courses of roughly equivalent length, the dura-

Duration
of courses

tion of a course being the total number of scheduled hours of instruction devoted to that course, whether those hours are concentrated as a single block of time or distributed in multiple brief sessions over a number of weeks or months. Even in curricula where mastery of objectives is the primary consideration, however long it takes the student, there is still the notion of a definite period of time that should be sufficient for most students to achieve the desired mastery. This notional time may then be used for planning purposes to indicate the "length" of each course. It may well be necessary, when packaging objectives, to juggle whole chains and segments of chains so as to achieve an acceptable length for every course. The time factor becomes even more important when student performance is to be evaluated at the end of each course, for few students or faculty will tolerate the strain of successive, full-scale, certifying evaluations over a brief period of time just because certain courses are, in their view unnecessarily, short.

A second factor affecting the delimitation of courses is the inevitable occurrence of the same objective in more than one chain. The question then arises whether to allocate that objective to one course only, and make that course the first one of the set to be presented, or whether to include the objective in more than one course but *specify an increasing level of expectation* each time it reappears. The choice will depend partly on the nature of the objective and partly on the difficulties encountered in sequencing courses when multiple objectives are common to several chains of objectives.

It may be helpful to look briefly at the matter of an allocation of curricular time for studies not commonly thought of as course work, for instance electives, research projects, independent study time, integrative

Time for
non-course
studies

sessions. If we accept the definition of a course as a specific collection of objectives (purposes), and if we then ask ourselves to specify the purposes served by the provision of curricular time for electives and other activities, there is no reason why we should not regard these kinds of studies as simply other courses. They will have their specific stated objectives, their scheduled curricular time, perhaps some form of instruction or active supervision, and often an ongoing evaluation of student performance, official or unofficial. Regarded in this way, they take their place with standard courses in the normal way of planning. While it may be objected that such matters as electives and research activities will inevitably occupy much more of the student's time than the meagre curricular hours allocated for them, it may equally be said that students will inevitably spend much more time on course work than the hours scheduled for lectures, laboratory sessions, ward-rounds, and so on. There is no essential difference.

A number of extraneous considerations may affect decisions regarding the establishment of courses. For example, it may be that a school has outstanding strength in a particular field of studies that would normally form only part of a course. A powerful inducement is then present to expand that segment into a full course. Another instance is that of a new discipline or field of study perceived to be emerging, which should be included somewhere within the curriculum, perhaps as an independent course. These matters require full and widely representative discussion before a final decision is taken.

It is now necessary to determine how the courses are to be placed in sequence, to give the total curriculum a sense of progression and to provide for the student as he moves through it a sense of growing competence.

Sequencing the Courses

The placing of courses in sequence is not a task to be approached empirically, for there are principles governing the organization of separate curricular parts into an optimal programme. These are briefly discussed at this point.

The Principles

The first principle is that of *repetition*. If a student is to understand and be able to apply certain concepts, then repeated opportunities for understanding and for application have to be provided. Otherwise those concepts will be driven out by more recent learning and the student will forget what he has initially gained: not only the skills of application but the very concepts as well.

It is evident that those concepts or skills which are most widely applicable, and those essential to an understanding of complex relationships, should appear amongst the earliest components of an educational programme. This brings us to the second principle in ordering components, that of *increasing complexity*. Repetition by itself serves memory to some extent but it should be used, wherever possible, in combination with an ever-increasing challenge to the student's ability to manipulate the concept or improve the skill involved and apply it in more and more complex situations. In this way repetition is changed from mechanical exercise to constant stimulus, with benefit to application as well as memory.

Finally, it should be possible to arrange curricular components in such a way that the resulting juxtaposition of components will assist the students' learning by the *correlation* of one with another. Thus the development by students of a professional skill is regarded as more efficient when it is accompanied by the learning of desirable attitudes related to that skill. Again, the application of the principle of correlation is illustrated in medical curricula by the development of the body-system courses wherein structure, function and development, both normal and abnormal, of a body-system are presented to the student as closely together as possible in time.

These three principles are not absolute imperatives without which no programme is possible, but to ignore them is to make the learning extremely difficult for the student. They are guidelines to be followed; the more completely they can be followed the more effectively the programme is likely to function. They can be applied at various stages in curricular planning, though the most obvious application is at the course-planning level. For an expansion of these concepts see Tyler (1949).

Sequencing usually includes placing some courses in parallel as well as others in series. Having courses in parallel allows a change of pace, setting, content and instructors, forestalling or minimizing monotony for the learner and allowing faculty and other instructors, particularly those engaged in professional practice, to devote at least part of their day to other necessary activities.

The Practice

Application of the above principles to sequencing can be difficult; it has been said that logically every course should come first. It is probably true that any given course can be placed first, with the proviso that the only assumptions made concerning students at the start of the course are those associated with admission to the programme. Those apart, every expectation of student performance will be an objective of the first course. This means that since everything is new the first course will be longer, perhaps much longer, than the same course would be if placed later in the programme. It also implies that the very last course will be "trim", since all duplicate objectives will have been introduced previously and the number of *new* concepts and principles will be minimal.

The further implication, and an important one, is that any future change in the order of courses must involve much more than a switch of current blocks of time. The assumptions concerning students starting a course do not remain the same when the course is moved to another position in the curriculum; the list of preceding courses will not be the same, so the starting point of the course will change. In addition, for the course that is moved to an earlier position, certain duplicate objectives may now have to be introduced for the first time, whereas with the previous sequence it could be assumed that they had already been met.

The sequence of courses that is finally worked out will have as its basis some rationale or organizing principle, stated or not, which served to guide the group towards its decision and made sense of that particular sequence. This organizing principle should be made known to students and faculty in some way, perhaps in an introductory document on the curriculum or in the very first course document.

We now have a total set of objectives packaged into courses which are arranged in a particular sequence. The next step is to allocate instructional time for each individual course.

Allotting Course Time

A curriculum normally has assigned to it a total elapsed time and a total allotted instructional time. For example, a law school curriculum takes three academic years to complete, each year containing about 25 hours of instructional time per week for 40 weeks, a total approximating 1000 hours of instructional time per year. In a similar way estimates can be made of elapsed and allotted times for medical, nursing and other professional curricula.

When the total instructional time is known, a reasonable method for a first attempt at distributing the time between courses is to base it on the number of objectives per course, or on the number of objectives perceived to be major ones. In this way a first approximation of the required instructional time is provided, to be altered as found necessary in the light of experience in presenting the courses. Such alteration, however, must be authorized only by the group charged with responsibility for the entire curriculum, and not left to power bargaining among department heads, course chairmen or teaching committees. For the moment, this provisional allocation gives the faculty designing the curriculum an opportunity to divide into course committees, ready to design in greater detail the nature and content of each course.

The Individual Course

Overall Organization

It was mentioned above that the courses forming the curriculum were identified and placed in sequence through the use respectively of an organizing element (for continuity) and an organizing principle (for sequence). Within each individual course there is also the need to identify organizing elements and principles.

As an example of the former, a course in torts in a law school curriculum can be taught using either of two different themes or organizing elements, both quite legitimate logically and educationally. One theme is the reiteration of the development of tort law as a manifestation of *Organizing element* social concern about remedying wrongs and the other is the reiteration of tort law as a growing body of precedent using court decisions as they occurred in common law. In medicine, a course in the physical examination of the patient can use reiteration of the concept of the physician as data-gatherer, with instrumentation available to help him in the process. An alternative is the reiteration of the concept of monitoring the functioning of the body, with frequent checking in the different body-systems for the effectiveness of that functioning.

As an example of an organizing principle, a course in legal interviewing can be so organized that the sequence of experiences goes from interviewing the client (obtaining basic information) to counselling the client *Organizing principle* (placing the collected information against the law and thus informing the client about possible actions) to negotiation (enabling the lawyer to negotiate, with his client, possible actions they can take either together or one on behalf of the other). To use a medical example, in a course in medicine providing an overview of the psychopathologies the latter can be introduced in a sequence that reflects the order of the various components of the mental status review. They can also be taught in the order of increasing incidence as met with in physicians' offices. There are many organizing principles available to faculties of professional schools; they only await discovery, selection and adoption.

Teaching Units

The objectives of the course can now be divided into smaller groups, the teaching units. Each is composed of a closely-knit subset of the course objectives which the planners recognize as most efficiently learned in contiguity. Courses usually consist of about five to ten units, although there are no set limits.

In planning a teaching unit there are many questions that must be decided by the unit planners. To begin with, what is the place of the unit in the course? This question may be subdivided into three component questions. *General Organization* What prerequisite knowledge, skills and attitudes are the students assumed to have attained prior to starting the unit? What previous learning needs to be reiterated or built upon in the present unit? What later learning in the course contains the assumption that specific objectives of the present unit have been achieved by the students? These must all be identified and included in the right place in curricular planning.

What is unique about this unit? Are the unique elements of the unit to be brought out by instructors or instead left for the students to discover? We recommend that whatever is unique *should* be highlighted and made into the core of the unit, so that other learning can be built on it.

Which organizing elements and organizing principles are to be chosen to weave the parts of the unit together? That which is perceived as the core of the unit can often be used as the organizing element, providing continuity to the unit. As for organizing principles, those most often used are: simple to complex, theory to practice, normal to abnormal.

What is the level of instruction to be, and which teaching formats are to be used in the unit? Will the planned instruction be at the right level for the students, not beyond their capabilities but difficult enough to challenge *Level of instruction* them? If the objectives of the unit are complex, or high in the Bloom taxonomy, then more time than usual will have to be given to instruction. With skills as objectives, sufficient time has to be built into the unit to permit the practice of those skills, together with repeated feedback to students individually as they become increasingly proficient. With attitudes and values as objectives, time is needed for each student to comprehend what these attitudes and values are, as demonstrated by those instructors he admires, and then, in imitation of them, to assume and manifest these attitudes in order to see how compatible they are with his own set of values and attitudes.

Given the objectives selected for the unit, what are the best methods of learning and of teaching to be applied so that students may best attain those objectives? The reader is referred to Chapter 6, and to Appendix C where *Methods of learning & teaching* possible teaching methods are displayed appropriate to the types of objectives developed. Is it going to be possible to provide a mix of learning activities and instructional techniques that will prevent boredom from setting in? And what opportunities are to be provided for students to learn through association, by studying not only knowledge but also its application at the same time? A detailed discussion of the principles of instructional design can be found in Gagne and Briggs (1979).

What resources should be available to the instructors in this course? Do we need patients, or clients? What space and equipment are required to help students learn? For example, how much space is needed for formal group *Resources needed* discussions arising out of lecture content, or for instruction requiring laboratory demonstrations or practice in bench and clinical research? What other resources are available locally? What learning materials need to be handed out to students prior to the beginning of the unit?

Printed resource materials often pose problems to the instructors. Sometimes no one is comfortable with the course text, since it does not match the unit's objectives. In such cases the text may need to be supplemented, for example by printed hand-outs. There is also the question of the logical structure of the relevant chapters. Does it match the rationale the instructors want to use in covering the same content? If not, how do the students learn to put the two rationales together, or to choose one over the other? Instruction bridging the two conceptual frameworks will have to be provided, either by newly written materials or by lectures in scheduled class time. Is the text up-to-date? Sometimes concepts and principles, even facts, become dated within a very short time of the original publication date. Sometimes conventions in professional circles are altered, requiring measurements, formulas, equations, constants, and normal values, to be expressed in other numbers and other units than in the past. If some principles and theories are controversial, to what extent should students be brought into the controversy? Does the controversy involve the unit's instructional staff? If so, which side is to be supported for purposes of professional instruction? Does the depth of current knowledge of the students make any difference in coming to a decision?

One of the more difficult tasks is that of selecting instructors for the individual sessions of the unit. All may represent expertise; but the question of their ability to lecture, to lead small group discussion, to provide a professional role model, also deserves an answer. *Choice of instructors* Which instructors are available who meet minimal criteria of selection such as knowing their subject, presenting their topic well, teaching in a relaxed manner and seeming to be completely comfortable with student questions? There may well be a place for short courses or quick workshops on teaching methods which can be of considerable benefit to the instructors assigned to a unit.

Students need feedback on their learning. Therefore a decision must be made on what learning evaluations will be offered to them, to provide that feedback. Some feedback will be informal, by questions from the instructors to the students to determine if they understand *Learning evaluations* the topics at hand. Sometimes students want a more formal evaluation, one that mimics the coming certifying evaluation at the end of the unit or the end of the course, or the annual comprehensive examinations covering the same territory.

Finally, the unit needs to be put together on paper, to see if answers to all the above questions have been found. This first schedule will give warning if there is an imbalance in the allotment of time to various components of the unit. The unit's instructional time must fit into the time slots made available to the group doing the planning. Clear commitments have to be obtained from instructors for their teaching time. A failure to appear because of conference conflicts is a violation of the teaching contract in higher education, and should be treated seriously. The unit's plans will have to be collated with those for other units in the same course, and problems of articulation between units solved, so that a course plan can develop.

The Blueprint for Instruction

The final step in the long process of curricular design is the development of a total blueprint for instruction. This will consist of a series of documents, organized by course, so that each course document contains a study guide, a schedule of instruction, and a statement concerning assessment.

A. The study guide

The study guide consists of:

1. An overview of the course. This is a brief description of the scope of the course, its particular emphasis and basic themes, and its organization as a series of linked segments, that is, the curriculum units.

2. A list of appropriate learning facilities, organized by units. These facilities include the schedule of instruction, see Section B below.

3. The method of ordering the learning, or the organizing principle(s) used in the course.

4. A statement of assumptions about entering students. This usually contains a reminder of prerequisite objectives (and an identification of the curriculum units in previous courses that addressed those objectives), a restatement of particular concepts introduced in previous courses and now needing to be reviewed, and a note of particular skills required on entering the course.

5. A statement of objectives for the course.   Objectives may be presented in a number of ways. One way is to give examples of the types of medical or nursing or legal problems that the student will be expected to manage on completion of the course, together with a statement of the kinds of knowledge required to attempt their proper management and an indication of the minimally acceptable level of competence. Another way of presenting objectives is to list the requirements in behavioural terms and to provide references to the content that the student should master for adequate performance of those behaviours. Regardless of the way objectives are presented, the essential feature is to communicate clearly to faculty and students alike how the student is to perform.

6. Optimally, cases or problems on which students can individually and in groups test their attainment of the objectives.

7. References, including recommended texts, articles, names of appropriate resource faculty.

Although written by the teaching faculty of that course for use by students taking the course, the guide is obviously of use also to participating faculty and to those in charge of the total curriculum as the definitive statement of intent by the course instructors.

B. The schedule of Instruction

This is very important since it not only gives a notice of events but, by the sequence of topics, can give the students some indication of the organizing principle(s) that are being used to hold the course together. The schedule lists minimally:

1. The teaching sessions in chronological order, with the times for each session stated.

2. The general theme or topic of each session.

3. The mode of instruction used in each session, for example, lecture, small-group discussion, laboratory session, or tutorial. The main reason for including this information is that students prepare differently for certain types of learning related to the mode of instruction.

4. The location of each session.

5. The names of instructional staff involved in each session.

6. Needs for special equipment for every session, such as a projector, microscopes, examining rooms with one-way mirrors for observation, display cases, and so on.

C. The Statement Concerning Assessment

A broad indication is given of the recommended formats of assessment for the course, together with a statement of time to be allotted to assessment. Thus, a course in medicine may have an assessment session at its close consisting of a one-hour peripatetic examination, a two-hour written examination of one hundred multiple-choice questions plus five short-answer questions, and a half-hour demonstration of a skill by the students. In law, assessment may consist of a term paper of around thirty pages on a selected topic, to be completed during the course, and a final examination of three hours' duration consisting of the analysis of cases and thirty multiple-choice questions.

All of the work described in the last few chapters requires the efficient use of human resources. In the next chapter we turn to a consideration of the most effective means of organizing a faculty group to proceed with curriculum construction and revision.

Chapter 12

IMPLEMENTING THE DESIGN

In previous chapters we have been concentrating on the concepts and procedures of curriculum, course and unit development. We have said very little, though, about the faculty activity required to bring about a new or revised and renovated curriculum. It is at this point that we turn our attention to what one might call the political side of curriculum construction.

In the last analysis the development or revision of a curriculum becomes the responsibility of a dedicated group of individuals, of faculty members, who will provide the co-ordination and direction of the task to maximum benefit and who will be considered the educational master planning group of the professional school. Its responsibility will be global and the work will be pressing.

Setting up the Master Planning Group

Size of Group

What size of group is likely to be most effective? The group should be large enough to provide a variety of backgrounds of academic interest and experience that can be capitalized upon by the group in making its decisions. At the same time it should not be made too large in an attempt to accommodate a multiplicity of interests, for then its representativeness suggests to each member that the specialized interest he represents should take precedence over the general interest of the school. Rather, group members need to consider themselves a corporate entity, openly and unreservedly discussing issues and procedures with the same end in view. This means understanding each other clearly and relating freely to one another.

The results of extensive research during the 1940s in the field of group dynamics suggest that the optimal number for such a working-and-sharing group be around six or seven. Six seems to be the maximum number of people that a person can openly relate to and keep clearly in mind as a collection of individuals (Berelson & Steiner 1964). A minimum of five, however, is recommended, for if the group is smaller than this it will be seen by other faculty members as too powerful a group for its size and it will engender more skepticism or even suspicion about its decisions than it truly warrants.

Selection of Members

How should the members of this group, which we may call the Curriculum Committee, be selected? In answer, one general principle is that the representation should be as broad as possible among *concerned* constituencies.

Faculty and students Certainly faculty members should be in the Curriculum Committee, but then so should students, for students have a unique and significant contribution to make in the planning stages either as consumers of the current programme or as potential consumers of the new programme. Particularly in a new school, student input is invaluable for in no school is the total planning completed prior to the entry of the first class. Even before the first class arrives, some form of student representation may be solicited from the pre-professional years in other faculties, from certain graduate students in selected programmes or from recent graduates of professional schools elsewhere who are continuing their education locally or who have just taken up practice in the area.

Administrators of profession-related institutions and services in the community constitute a concerned group, possessing executive skills and talents based on an understanding of management concepts that is unusual

Administrators of related institutions among general faculty but extremely useful to any major planning group. Hospital and local health agency administrators are examples in the medical field, Bar Examination Course instructors and private and government lawyers for law, nursing association officers and head matrons (or vice-presidents for nursing services, as they are becoming known) for nursing, and corporate executives for management. These administrators take their appointments to planning groups seriously for, before agreeing to serve, they review most carefully the implications of commitment and interest that guarantee their central involvement in curricular planning for professional programmes.

There are obvious political considerations to be taken into account in the selection process, as individual members have various professional and academic affiliations. In a new school in a new location, for example, one *A local* of the respected and trusted local practitioners will al- *practitioner* most certainly be a member of the Curriculum Commit- tee. He knows his way around the professional community and he can interpret it to the school, and vice versa. This con- cept may also have merit where a substantial change is envisioned in an ex- isting curriculum. Within the school there must be a balance of perceived powers. This suggests, for example, that members of the Committee will be representative of various faculty age-groups and academic ranks, for the Committee's decisions will have to be adopted by the general faculty, with *Internal* or without persuasion. In addition, in a professional *balance* school there tend to be broad interests that keep a wary eye on one another so that none of them becomes power- ful enough to distort some generally acceptable balance between them. Faculty supporting these various interests must feel that their particular af- filiation is effectively represented at the planning stage.

Group Characteristics

The Curriculum Committee will, one hopes, collectively possess certain characteristics. No one member is expected to have them all, but each characteristic must be exhibited by at least one person in the group if the latter is to function effectively. The efficacy of small groups is a function partly of their ability to share ideas and partly of the talent some individuals possess for seeing the implications, both theoretical and practical, of ideas proposed by others. Some people appear to be highly analytical in their thinking. Others, whether through conscious training or unconscious as- similation, have learned to be adept at synthesis. They are able to put ideas together in new ways and to realize the theoretical and practical consequen- ces. The Curriculum Committee requires all these skills in its corporate membership.

Since the group will be organizing an educational plan it must be knowledgeable about how people learn, particularly at the post-secondary level. Over the years students have achieved a deeper understanding of how *Know* teaching should assist learning and, as a consequence, *how* they are more demanding than were students of a decade *people* or two ago in their expectations of the teaching ability *learn* of university instructors. The droning lecture, the ill- prepared laboratory exercise, the practice-session downgraded to a demonstration, these simply will not do, regardless of who is paying the tuition. Attitudes toward laboratory experiments in the health sciences, for example involving the "needless" sacrifice of animals, have changed laboratory exercises to such an extent that very few are now conducted. The relevant experiment is seen to be that of attempting to help the patient through diagnostic and therapeutic regimens. These are among the factors suggesting that group members must have a good working knowledge of how people learn.

Those involved in planning should, as a group, have a knowledge of how people work effectively together. They should be skilled in oral and written communication and be able to apply principles of group dynamics *Know how* in their work with one another, and with other commit-*people work* tees, on common problems affecting the curriculum *together* (Johnson & Johnson 1982). As the educational plan grows through the development of a basic set of principles and procedures, and as the Curriculum Committee becomes more experienced in planning, the more it will be able to identify the best routes for making progress and for avoiding obstacles.

Individual Abilities

Group members should be selected for the individual abilities they will bring to the work. Some will be selected on the basis of evident talent, some on experience shared with colleagues and some on the basis of their potential service to the school and its programme.

Effective planners, however, also have certain personal characteristics that are attitudinal. They are able to stand back and take a broad look at the whole educational programme with detachment. Each member views the *Broad* curriculum as a whole and regards the interests of his *outlook* own discipline as taking second place to the primary interests of the total curriculum. One anticipates that they will each have considerable skill in the translation of concepts into other terms and other ideas. Most of the members will be able to do this for their own disciplines but now it has to be done with the concepts underlying the new curriculum (Ausubel 1964; Schwab 1964). With any new idea there is an immediate problem in communication until others learn to feel at home with the new structure. To help them feel comfortable requires the art of persuasion. Most of us are skeptics when it comes to new ideas but our skepticism can be reduced or even eliminated by good argument. Persuasion is a most valuable personal skill.

There is a good deal of rough-and-tumble in educational deliberations and, with ideals so tightly intertwined with the realities of practice in the developing or revising of a school programme, things are often said enthusiastically but bluntly and without thought of their impact on the lis-

Avoid giving or taking offence
tener. So many interesting things are occurring in the work at hand that those deeply involved are using most of their energies to solve curricular problems. Comments are task-oriented, not person-oriented, and so not intended to be taken personally. By the same token the response to such comments is to address the argument, not the person, avoiding either taking or giving offence.

Those who thrive on the excitement of their group developing and controlling curricular change, and who are successful in their work, are quite realistic about themselves. They are able to evaluate their own contribu-

Realistic in self-evaluation
tions to the group objectively, accepting that what may seem like a great idea to one person may seem less than relevant to another because of their differing orientations to the work. Only discussion of ideas put forward will bring about some common understanding, while outright rejection of single contributions to the work of the group is self-defeating; but acceptance of the need for discussion, and tolerance in discussion, take patience all round

Once a decision has been reached by the group on any topic, particularly one that has engendered much debate and revealed widely differing points of view, it is important both to the morale of the group and to its ef-

Accept group decisions
fectiveness that this decision be accepted by all and that action based upon it be tolerated, if not actively promoted, by every member. Effective planners accept that you win some battles and you lose some; those you lose may perhaps be recovered at a future time but not until after those decisions have been put into effect and their consequences analysed.

Credibility of the Group

The tentative membership of the group, based on the considerations described above, has then to be looked at as a whole for an assessment of its overall credibility. In particular, the question must be asked whether decisions bearing the authority of the group on crucial matters known to be controversial are likely to be supported by the general faculty. If that is so, then this tentative membership can be confirmed.

One of the committee members selected will, aside from the general characteristics mentioned above, have the trust of senior school staff and the respect of his academic colleagues. If he has a clear and proper vision of the future of the school then he will make the best chairman. Whether he is nominated to his position of leadership by the senior executive group in an existing school or by the founding dean in a new school, once appointed he will in particular need to be a free agent beholden to no individual or group, an open communicator, and one who is able to see a clear track ahead through the maze of committee activity.

Focussing on Essential Tasks

Once the Curriculum Committee has been selected and a chairman installed, it is ready to focus on essential tasks. There is a danger that it will see itself not only in a leadership role in curricular development but also in an *executive* role, performing all planning and implementing functions itself. The assumption of this degree of leadership and involvement can result only in political catastrophe. Over-centralization of authority and responsibility results in decreased general activity. On the one hand, decisions take longer to make as every one of them must be referred to the central group; and on the other hand, a sense of urgency is lost in subordinate groups as they do not feel any personal responsibility for the decisions.

Overview of Total Activities

The total activities for which the Curriculum Committee is responsible, and from which it will select those that the Committee itself must undertake, consist of planning, implementing and reviewing the curriculum. These will be discussed in turn.

Planning a curriculum, as we have seen, is carried out in a number of stages. The first is the determination of broad outlines, deciding what kind of curriculum it is going to be. The term "curricular design" is used for this *Planning* general framework. The second stage of planning is the creation of a blueprint for instruction, based on the curricular design. The blueprint informs both faculty and students, in all necessary detail, of the instruction that will be offered and of the learning that is intended to be achieved. The third stage, also derived from the curricular design, is the development of an overall design for assessment of student performance. The fourth stage is production of a blueprint for this assessment. The final stage is the development of a programme of evaluation of the curriculum.

Implementing the curriculum consists mainly of presenting, according to the timetable contained in the blueprint, those aids to learning that are *Implementing* specified or implied in the blueprint for instruction. It includes the provision of faculty instructors at set times and places, as well as various means for self-instruction, and the allocation of materials, space and equipment that support these activities. Similarly it includes assessment of student performance according to the blueprint for this function, together with provision of the necessary personnel and facilities.

Finally, reviewing the curriculum includes review of both the planning and the implementation as defined above. It implies monitoring on an ongoing basis as well as holding periodic set reviews of individual curricular

Reviewing   segments and of the curriculum as a whole. The reader might assume that the process of review would be ongoing and automatic but, in actuality, this step is infrequently taken by educational institutions or component faculties. Consequently the review is often given over to some external agency in the hope that its detachment will guarantee objectivity, though it often guarantees lack of understanding of problems as well. Curricular bodies should assume responsibility for reviewing their own work regardless of whom else might be interested in the process; such review is educational and instructive! Recommendations for change by those who know, having been through the battles of curricular development, carry particular weight with general faculty who often have to vote such recommendations into official decisions and then carry them out.

Selecting its own Tasks

To know what to delegate and what to pursue on its own the Curriculum Committee will have, as its first task, the identification of those activities which it must itself conduct.

The production of a curricular design is an activity which the Curriculum Committee must, for obvious reasons, itself undertake. No other significant step in the educational programme can, or should, be taken until this first step has been largely accomplished. The development of a blueprint for instruction based on this design may, where the total number of faculty is small and likely to remain so, be attempted by the Curriculum Committee. However, the magnitude of the task, the varied professional expertise required and the time that must be devoted to the enterprise make it almost inevitable that the task be delegated to successive layers of subcommittees. The Curriculum Committee will then confine itself for the most part to monitoring the activities of the subcommittees that it has appointed, and helping these when necessary. Implementation of the blueprint is of necessity delegated.

In regard to the assessment of student performance, its design is again the business of the Curriculum Committee. The blueprint for this assessment is the concern of faculty at large and is therefore delegated, except when the total number of faculty is small. The function of implementation is also a matter for the faculty as a whole and therefore is delegated. Review of the curriculum is preferably carried out by the Curriculum Committee, though in some cases it may be convenient or prudent to delegate this task.

In summary, the Curriculum Committee will itself produce a design for the curriculum and a design for the assessment of student performance. Depending on the circumstances it may be forced, in addition, to construct the blueprint for instruction and the blueprint for assessment of student performance. It may reserve for itself the conduct of curricular reviews. All other functions will be delegated.

Overlap of Ongoing Activities

Over the course of the succeeding months the Curriculum Committee may find itself planning one part of the curriculum, implementing another and possibly even reviewing a third, all as concurrent activities. This is almost certain to occur in a new school, where the initial class usually arrives before the planning is anywhere near completion. It will be true whether some of these tasks are delegated or not, since the final responsibility for all of them lies with the Committee. It is faced not only with monitoring and controlling these activities but also with deciding the order in which they shall be carried out.

Setting up Derivative Groups

For each course, the Curriculum Committee sets up a derivative planning group, which may be called the course *sub*committee in order to emphasize its responsibility to the parent body. The senior group may decide to appoint all the members of the subcommittee as well as the chairman (or coordinator), or it may first select a chairman and then appoint the other members in consultation with the chairman. The latter method is more likely to result in a group whose members work well together.

The Chairman

The selection of a suitable course chairman at this early stage is almost as important as that of chairman of the Curriculum Committee discussed earlier, and for many of the same reasons: trust and respect, vision, and leadership ability. In addition the course chairman should be one who understands and is in sympathy with the educational goals and principles of the school and the selected instructional design, and who moreover is both willing and able to guide his colleagues on the subcommittee into working within the general guidelines provided by these concepts. It is imperative at this stage that the chairman possess expertise in some aspect of the course content, for without it he will not be accorded that professional respect which leads to the co-operation of his various colleagues and the willing acceptance of group decisions under his leadership.

The Membership

The initial membership of a course subcommittee should, if possible, include representatives of those interests likely to have the greatest need for instructional input to the course. In the case of a disciplinary course in medicine, for instance, such as a course in paediatrics or in anatomy, the various subspecialties in the discipline may be given representation on the course subcommittee: in the former case, general paediatrics, paediatric neurology, paediatric surgery, paediatric psychiatry, neonatology; in the latter, topographical anatomy, neuroanatomy, developmental anatomy, microanatomy. Not all of the subspecialties will carry equal instructional weight, depending on the special interests of the faculty who teach in the discipline and their view of the relative importance of the subspecialties in a medical curriculum, so that only some of the subspecialties need be represented on the subcommittee.

In the case of an interdisciplinary course, such as a respiratory system course, those disciplines expected to contribute most to instruction in the course will be represented on the subcommittee: for example internal medicine, physiology, anesthesiology, pathology. For the membership of an interdisciplinary course subcommittee it becomes important to select persons who are prepared to subordinate their disciplinary enthusiasms to the broader interests of the whole course, emphasizing the total system. In addition, the general principles of selecting group members, delineated earlier, are equally applicable to the selection of course subcommittee members.

Educating the Group

It is instructive, as well as beneficial, for every member of the subcommittee in turn to lead in the exercise of making his colleagues on the subcommittee justify their opinions and proposals. His role then is to assist the others in considering each proposal from the point of view of the student or practitioner, for whom competence in the content of this course is a necessary condition for the next stage of his formal education or for the independent practice of medicine. The questions constantly in each committee member's mind should be: "Is the student required to know or do at this stage whatever item is being proposed, in order to proceed to a subsequent stage?" and "Is this the most appropriate place in the curriculum for the student to learn this item?"

Discussion of questions of this kind in committee, among persons who are willing to listen as well as talk, can be a most effective, though initially disturbing, educational experience for committee members. Given suitable guidance by the chairman, however, there is no better way for the committee to have the educational principles and the educational objectives of the school sink in and be discovered as "real" forces that direct education, instead of their being regarded as theoretical castles-in-the-air that men of action feel it their duty to ignore. It is here, at the level of the course subcommittee, that the first major test of purposes and principles occurs, and the entire direction of the curriculum depends on the outcome.

Students as Members

What about the presence of students on a teaching subcommittee? Recent graduates as well as current students should be represented, since they were, or are, actively involved in the process as consumers. In an ongoing programme they can discuss the match between expectations and practice, with implications for revision of the blueprint. If a school has as yet no current students, one or two students can perhaps be borrowed from a neighbouring institution on a consultative basis. What will they do? They can be set to work constructing or reconstructing parts of the blueprint. They can comment on proposed changes in the blueprint submitted by other committee members, using practicality as a criterion.

Results of Decentralization

This decentralizing of decision making has a major advantage: the discussions and arguments that ensue among subcommittee members serve to educate them about the nature of the educational programme to which they are committed. On the other hand this advantage applies only to the initial membership. As subcommittee membership changes with time there is a tendency for new members, who are not as familiar as were the original faculty with the new or modified educational philosophy of the school, to recycle through the old discussions and to arrive at different conclusions, depending on the practices of the schools from which they graduated or from which they have recently been recruited.

Other disadvantages of this kind of decentralization include the possibility of two or more subcommittees selecting the same objective, resulting in unnecessary duplication of faculty effort and misuse of student and faculty time; the inadvertent omission of an important objective or topic from the curriculum because none of the subcommittees discussed it, resulting in a curricular gap; the wide variation in style of the statements of objectives issued by the different subcommittees; and the extensive time demanded of many faculty on many subcommittees rather than of a small number of faculty on a single committee.

In defence of this extensive time commitment by many of the faculty it may be argued that even the preparation of detailed objectives for the entire curriculum is too large a task for a single small committee, especially as a small group of faculty cannot command the range of professional expertise that the task requires. Against this view it may be contended that, in considering any single area of the curriculum, the faculty members of this small committee constitute an involved and broadly knowledgeable group with each member able to think above and beyond his own discipline, a group that can call on the appropriate expertise whenever necessary by delegation, co-operation, special invitation, appointment to membership of a task force, or other means. Decisions in each area of the curriculum will then be made, although on the basis of recommendations of the area experts, by "generalists"; for example, in medicine an internist member of the committee is a generalist when it comes to discussing orthopaedic matters, and a neuropathologist is a generalist when the organization of health care systems is the subject under consideration. In this way, the interests of the total curriculum may be broadened and any undue influence of a specialty diminished.

Setting Terms of Reference of Subcommittees

The reason for setting up a course subcommittee is that it shall plan that course. Later it will probably be required to carry the plan into effect and then modify it as necessary.

The above statement of initial purpose of subcommittees, however, has to be expanded by the Curriculum Committee into more specific terms of reference. In part, this is because the planning of different courses has certain elements in common; a list of these elements presented as terms of reference to course subcommittees will save all of them the time they would otherwise spend in deriving the list for themselves. It will also ensure that no major element is omitted from consideration. In addition, specific terms of reference are likely to deter a subcommittee from concentrating its energies on a single part of its work simply because this part is the easiest one to accomplish, or the most attractive, or because it produces results quickly. Its focus will remain broad.

Refine The Objectives

One of the terms of reference of every teaching subcommittee is to define in detail the objectives of its particular course, that is, the expected behaviours and appropriate content. Some or most of these may already have been determined (with various degrees of specificity) by the Curriculum Committee during its design stage of planning, when it divided the total time and objectives of the curriculum into courses. If that is the case, then the business of the subcommittee is to complete the task. If not, the Curriculum Committee will probably allocate to each course subcommittee a curricular segment such as (in medicine) "clinical psychiatry", or "the reproductive system", or "medical problem-solving I", or "growth and development", and it will require the subcommittee to start from scratch in working out the appropriate behaviours and content. This latter is the more cumbersome and time-consuming method.

Whichever method is used to define objectives, the accomplishment of this task involves the subcommittee both in academic decisions about what should be included and what should be left out, and in political decisions about overlap of courses and the boundary between one course and another. The first kind of decision is a matter for its independent judgement, and will result from a group consensus or more likely from the striking of compromises among its members. The second kind requires negotiation with other course subcommittees or an appeal to the senior committee for its advice or ruling.

When determined, the detailed course objectives are published for the benefit of students and faculty alike.

Establish Optimal Conditions

A second term of reference for every course subcommittee is to establish optimal preliminary conditions for achieving course purposes. This may involve consultation with affiliated groups and with other faculty within the university. An initial liaison will already have been established between the senior administrators of the professional school and various private and public institutions and voluntary agencies. It is now the task of the course subcommittee to strengthen that liaison into a working relationship and to form new liaisons as appropriate. For example, a mandatory period of apprenticeship of students to approved practitioners, as in the legal profession, demands a very close and communicative relationship with the group of practitioners within the local area.

It is entirely possible that when related institutions operate autonomously their modes of operation will restrict a committee's freedom of action. In medicine, an autonomous hospital organized according to body-systems, with separate units for patients with disorders of the urinary, musculo-skeletal, cardiovascular and other systems, is likely to rule out consideration of block clinical teaching *by discipline*. A hospital where the patient's agreement to be available for purposes of teaching is actively sought on admission, or as soon after as possible, provides more opportunities for clinical study than one where such permission is not routinely requested or is asked perfunctorily. All of these kinds of basic conditions require attention simultaneously with the selection of modes of learning and with identification of needed resources, to be discussed later.

Organize the Learning

A third term of reference for each course subcommittee is the intellectual organization of learning within a given instructional design. This, it should be pointed out, is *not* concerned with modes of learning or with the resources considered necessary.

As an example, a clinical course in paediatrics might be organized on the basis of:

a.   the prevalence of illness; for example, by ensuring that common ailments are well represented in the sample of paediatric patients provided to the student;

or

b.   the spectrum of disease; for example, using a group of patients selected so as to demonstrate, with the minimum number of patients, the widest possible range of symptoms, physical signs, and disease-states to be met with in children;

or

c.   illnesses that are peculiarly paediatric; for example, using a group of patients demonstrating those illnesses which occur only in children, or which are in some significant respect different in children from otherwise identical illnesses in adults;

or

d.   patients appearing during a specified period of time in the paediatric ward of a tertiary care hospital;

or

e.   some preferred mix of these.

To take a body-system course as another medical example, say the alimentary system, this may be organized on the basis of:

a   the individual organs of this body-system;

or

b.   specific functions of the system;

or

c.   the types of disease processes that affect the system;

or

d.   the presenting symptoms of malfunction of various parts of the system;

or

e.   some combination of these.

Whatever basis is selected, the organization of the course requires the selection of a minimal number of models, for example, concepts, patients, functions, diseases, developmental processes, mechanisms, such that the *Economy of appropriate models* study of this small group of models will involve the student in a very wide variety of facts, ideas, skills, theories, problems and methods of tackling them, appropriate to this course. Study of the models will also require the student to pursue many of these facets in some detail and correlate them with the models studied in other systems.

Communicate Needs

Another term of reference for all course subcommittees is to determine the needs of their courses and refer them for appropriate action. To take just one example, there are frequently clinics, health agencies and community hospitals whose facilities, programmes and staff might with benefit be incorporated into a new nursing or medical educational programme. The existence and availability of these resources reduces the demand on the educational institution for space, persons and materials essential to the educational programme. When the required resources have been identified, this information must be transmitted to the appropriate office.

For a new school this is not the simple process it might appear to be, for at this stage of development it is likely that administrative processes are somewhat untidy. The informal contacts adequate for a small number of faculty will now be giving way to the more formal structure necessitated by increasing numbers of faculty, with areas of uncertainty at many points during the transition period. Who should receive a particular bit of information, how it should be transmitted and by whom, may require a certain ingenuity to decide. Nevertheless, it is well to keep in mind the fact that information is useless unless it reaches the point where it can affect the making or the carrying out of a decision.

The various terms of reference given above are common to all subcommittees; others may be added as appropriate by the Curriculum Committee. Any subcommittee may feel the need to expand its terms of reference, and this topic is discussed below.

Providing Support and Encouragement

If we assume that derivative planning groups for all curricular segments (course subcommittees) have been set up and provided with terms of reference and a time limit, we can expect that these groups, left to their own devices, will collectively produce within the allotted time a detailed plan for a curriculum that is in accordance with the philosophy of the school and with its educational principles. While this may indeed be the case, in reality every one of the groups can benefit from various forms of continuing support and encouragement in order to function well.

Ratifying Revised Terms of Reference

The first need for support arises as soon as a course subcommittee refines its terms of reference. The ones that have been provided to it constitute only those that are applicable to all subcommittees; each individual subcommittee may wish to amplify those terms and add others to suit its particular needs. Having done so, it will desire reassurance that these modified terms of reference are in order. It is then for the Curriculum Committee, or whoever issued the original terms of reference, to review the modifications and either formally accept them or assist the subcommittee to make those changes necessary to obtain formal sanction.

In those cases where a subcommittee is merely given a vague idea of its main function and invited to write its own terms of reference, formal sanction becomes particularly important. Permitting a derivative committee to write its own terms of reference and then act on them without reference back to the parent committee can be fraught with danger and is not recommended, although it occurs in most schools at one time or another. The potential for harm can be greatly reduced or eliminated by the simple precaution just described.

Maintaining Liaison

As the subcommittees pursue their tasks, developing new ways of handling old problems and of working their way around new problems, the activities of different subcommittees begin to diverge. The chairman of each group *Informal* tends to feel that his group is, by itself, charting un-*liaison* known and treacherous waters. He is unsure at times of the direction in which they are moving and not always persuaded of the suitability of every member of his crew. Progress may be rapid at times and inspire confidence, at other times slow or circular with associated bickering and despondency. In these early stages, before sufficient progress has established confidence, it is necessary that the Curriculum Committee maintain a fairly close liaison with the chairman of each subcommittee.

The liaison may be effected formally or informally. One possible way is for the chairman of the Curriculum Committee and all or some of the course chairmen to hold informal discussions at a working lunch once or twice a month. A valuable outcome of this liaison is that problems common to two or more subcommittees can often be identified, and it may then be discovered that a solution worked out by one subcommittee will provide the basis for solution by the others. There is some reassurance in learning that other groups are proceeding at approximately the same pace as one's own, and some stimulus in the knowledge that another group has progressed in some particular area even further than one's own group.

It is also helpful to subcommittee chairmen to discuss a special problem, or its suggested solutions, with other chairmen who are less immediately involved with the minutiae and the personalities concerned. Not *Formal* the least of the benefits of such liaison is the opportunity *liaison* to assess the extent to which decisions taken by the course subcommittees are in accordance with the intent of the curriculum, and to judge the degree of coherence in the development of the various courses. Particularly in the case of an unfamiliar kind of curriculum, as a student-oriented curriculum must seem to faculty used to an instructor-oriented curriculum, reassurance is frequently sought to confirm that the steps being taken are in the right direction and constitute a valid, practical derivation from curricular theory.

A complementary method of producing this liaison is to arrange for members of the Curriculum Committee to be invited to attend certain meetings of course subcommittees. Aside from assuring the subcommittees of the close and continuing interest of their parent body, these visits serve a number of other useful purposes. The functioning of each subcommittee can be observed by the visitor. The latter will note, for example, the effectiveness of the chairman in leading the discussions and guiding them to a close in an appropriate form of group decision; the chairman's ability to control the inveterate talkers and to encourage the naturally reticent; his determination in preventing or minimizing clashes of personality and in concentrating attention on the issues; and his persuasiveness in generating enthusiasm and in getting tasks accomplished on time.

When a chairman is unable to handle these and similar tasks well it is probable that his committee will flounder and soon cease to be productive. The visitor has then an opportunity to analyse the problem and initiate appropriate action. A word in private with the chairman may be sufficient, together with a subtle reinforcement of the chairman's authority in committee. Some form of incentive may be introduced to persuade a chairman to improve his leadership abilities, for example the provision of time and assistance to attend a workshop on this topic. In a very few cases, and as a last resort, it may be best to recommend a change of chairman.

At the same time the visitor has the opportunity to observe the other committee members in action, noting the one or two who always seem to come up with new ideas; the person who keeps the whole educational programme in mind; the individual who, though not officially chairman, in effect directs the meeting; the member who is good at criticizing the work of others but offers nothing constructive in its place; and the various talents shown by different members in the several tasks in hand. An accumulation of information of this sort from the different subcommittees and other groups provides the Curriculum Committee with valuable data, mostly concerning the different roles played by a faculty member in different settings. In a few cases the role may be consistent from one setting to another. Such information permits the Committee to employ faculty to its and their best advantage, thereby providing a suitable balance of committee memberships, competent committee leadership, and a reserve of persons with special abilities which can be focussed on areas of special difficulty when necessary. In addition it enables consistent strengths and weaknesses of individual faculty to be identified and encourages appropriate retraining.

Sanctioning the Work

As each major task of a subcommittee is completed it is usual to seek assurance that the work is acceptable. This is rarely, if ever, a matter of professional competence in the particular field of study. Rather it has to do with the placing of particular studies at certain stages or in a certain order, with the appropriateness of modes of learning and of instruction, with logistics or costs of materials, or the compatibility of scheduled activities with agreed educational principles and the declared purposes of the course. As these are decisions that ultimately are the prerogative of the Curriculum Committee it is important that the latter should formally pronounce itself satisfied with the work and so inform the subcommittee.

If a subcommittee has somehow gone astray it has a right to be told so, subject only to the condition that it will, on request, be assisted in its redirection. There is perhaps nothing as frustrating as being told that one's work is unsatisfactory or wrong, with no indication given of how it can be corrected or what it should look like when done properly, unless it be to find that the work has been reallocated to a colleague, with the implication that one is irremediable. When sanction is withheld it must be substituted by a combination of continuing redirection and encouragement until sanction is given.

Developing the Structure of Implementation

Those who are in charge of the planning process have to take into account the next stage beyond planning, namely the stage of implementation. Putting plans into effect is neither automatic nor effortless and, if it is to proceed smoothly, it requires a special organization of its own. Planning cannot be considered complete until the structure of implementation has been developed and established.

Implementation v. Planning Structures

This structure is different from that of the planning process in one major respect. Planning normally benefits from diverse opinions, different professional interests and previous experiences, with wide consultation and lengthy discussion often preceding decisions. Its structure is based on the assumption of group responsibility, open representation of interests and extensive consultative procedures. Planning takes place within a theoretical framework, and planning decisions are assumed to be expressions of the total group although they are commonly conveyed to other parts of the organization by individual group chairmen. Thus, in general, the responsibilities of a planning group member cannot be delegated. Implementation, on the other hand, is a practical exercise. What has to be done is already known in considerable detail, so that efficiency in getting it done assumes greater importance, if indeed it does not become the primary consideration. The structure of implementation is therefore based on individual responsibility, consultation is limited to those who can provide the requirements of personnel and materials or indicate their sources, and delegation of tasks is commonplace. In summary, planning is a group democratic process whereas implementation is an authoritarian individual process with that authority consciously delegated.

Lines of Authority

It follows that the structure of implementation is essentially a linear series of positions, each position directed from the one before and, in turn, directing the ones to follow.

Chief Executive

At the head of the line is a senior faculty position, for example that of Associate Dean of Education, the incumbent being responsible to the Dean for the implementation of the total curriculum. It might be considered appropriate that the chairman of the Curriculum Committee occupy this position of total responsibility for implementation, on the assumption that, once the planning for the first class has been completed, the planners have finished their assignment and can now turn their attention to implementation. The assumption, however, is incorrect for there is a need to retain the Curriculum Committee as a specific entity but with new functions.

In the first place this committee must exercise the important function of monitoring the curriculum in order to ensure that the foundations on which the curriculum was built are preserved. It is all too easy for multidisciplinary and interdisciplinary forms of teaching to be replaced by lectures, for free time to be eroded by unauthorized "optional" mini-courses, for students' work with patients to be replaced by instructors' demonstrations or by repetitive service work, and for examinations to proliferate and take on punitive aspects. To detect such aberrations at an early stage and to undertake remedial action are functions for which the Curriculum Committee ought to be responsible on a continuing basis.

In the second place, perfect planning is an ideal very rarely observed in practice; normally the initial plans have to be modified in the light of experience and changing resources. This process of modification occurs not once but repeatedly from year to year. When the planning for the first class has been completed each member of the Curriculum Committee is, indeed, enabled to spend significantly less time on planning and to devote a larger portion of his time to teaching, to research and to clinical service, but the function of curricular modification must be carried on.

Thirdly, if the chairman of the Curriculum Committee were to agree to accept total responsibility for implementation certain consequences would ensue. He must then, in his role as group chairman, work together with the Committee as one among equals but, in his other role as chief of implementation, either bypass the Committee or act as its master: a most uneasy situation. This duality of roles may not be handled confidently, thereby interfering with the workings of the Curriculum Committee, especially in those areas where the boundary between planning and implementation becomes fuzzy. The effect on faculty in general may be even more disturbing, as the duality of roles introduces a confusion in faculty's perception of the lines of authority and communication.

The position of responsibility for implementation of the total curriculum is therefore best filled by one who is not an active member of the Curriculum Committee. The need for this person to be thoroughly familiar with that which he must implement can be met by his appointment early in the planning stage and by his membership *ex officio* of the Curriculum Committee.

Course Chairmen

The immediate subordinates of the chief executive are the chairmen of the course subcommittees, who are individually responsible to him for the implementation of their various courses. As mentioned earlier, these chairmen are appointed by the Curriculum Committee, preferably in collaboration with the Associate Dean of Education.

It will be apparent that each course chairman assumes a duality of roles similar to that which was deprecated above, but two factors make this situation acceptable. One is the separation in time of the two roles. The planning role arises out of the review following each presentation of the course, when decisions are made regarding the nature of the changes, if any, that are to be made in the course for its next presentation; this is soon followed by revision of the blueprint. The implementing role begins following completion of the revisions to the blueprint. The separation in time between planning and implementation may not be absolute, but it is sufficient to effect a practical separation of the two roles.

The second factor that makes the duality acceptable is economy of manpower. It is one thing to add an extra person to the Dean's office with responsibility for implementing the curriculum, and quite another thing to add ten or fifteen faculty members to the existing course subcommittees with responsibility for implementing individual courses; the more so as these added faculty members will be expected, as a group, to possess expertise in the whole curriculum. The possible confusion of roles of course chairmen, with its attendant consequences, constitutes a burden that will seem acceptable in preference to such a seemingly profligate use of faculty. It will help in minimizing the confusion if each course chairman keeps two things clear: one, that in his planning role he is part of, and acts as spokesman for, one committee (the course subcommittee) which is collectively answerable to another committee (the Curriculum Committee); and two, that in his executive role he acts in an individual capacity and is personally answerable to another individual (the Associate Dean of Education).

Curriculum Unit Managers

In his executive role the course chairman directs a number of unit managers, generally a different manager for each unit, who are personally responsible to him for the implementation of their various units. Unit managers are appointed by the course subcommittee. Here again, practical considerations require that each unit be both planned and implemented by the same person. The same kind of potential for confusion exists at this level also, the unit manager being subordinate in his planning role to the course subcommittee but in his implementation role to the course chairman only. As in the previous case the two roles are normally separated in time.

Instructors

The unit manager in turn directs a number of instructors selected by him, each instructor personally responsible to him for implementing his particular part of the unit. At this the working level, so to speak, it is normally up to the individual unit manager to determine the extent to which his instructors shall be encouraged to participate in planning the unit. He is only required to ensure that they understand their parts in the unit, for example by explaining to them the purposes of the unit and the reasons for preferring a particular mode of instruction.

Staff Positions

The linear executive organization described above may have associated with it, and shared with other organizations within the Faculty, a number of staff positions or service groups whose assistance may be sought by one or many levels of the organization. An audio-visual unit is one example, an office of medical education is another. In non-disciplinary medical curricula special units may have to be set up to provide and maintain special collections, for example, anatomical and pathological materials and optical records of the clinical use of imaging techniques such as radiography. All of these service groups are responsible to the Associate Dean of Education insofar as their curricular functions are concerned.

Areas of Responsibility

The areas of executive responsibility should be clear from the above description. The Associate Dean is responsible to the Dean for implementation of the curriculum. Course chairmen are responsible to the Associate Dean for implementing their respective courses; and unit managers to the course chairman for implementing their various units. Instructors are responsible to the unit manager for carrying out their assigned instructional tasks in that unit.

Lines of authority run from Associate Dean to course chairmen, from each course chairman to his unit managers and from each unit manager to his group of instructors. Service groups normally respond to requests from any level, although they may in some circumstances appeal to the next higher level for confirmation of the request. Their authority derives directly from the Associate Dean and they are responsible to him.

Setting Time Limits

Complementing the structure of implementation is the provision of a timetable for completing the various parts of the instructional blueprint for the first class. Most curricula are sequential in that certain parts of them must be completed before other parts are begun, so that the timetable for completing the parts of the blueprint can also be sequential. The need for a timetable, and for pressure from the senior officials to adhere to the timetable, may be self-evident; but it appears that one cannot over-emphasize the point that *everything tends to take longer than anticipated.* One cannot enforce a deadline on creative thinking. It is possible, however, to influence the conditions under which that thinking takes place, such as by release of the faculty member from less essential duties, by provision of skilled assistance or by increasing motivation to complete the task.

Since most deadlines can be used only as guides they should be set so as to allow a wide margin of safety. When pressure to meet deadlines is applied from the early stages of planning, and optimal conditions are provided, there is a greater likelihood of avoiding the last-minute panic that occurs when the first class to use the new curriculum is well into its first year of studies and yet the details for the second year are not even within sight of completion. It is one of the tests of the leadership of the Faculty to arrange the stages of planning and implementation so that faculty, in addition to meeting their deadlines, will have had adequate time to discuss problems and issues thoroughly and to reach major decisions in an unhurried manner yet without causing delay.

This explication of the human side of curricular planning and implementation may seem to the casual reader to be inordinately detailed. Experience has taught us, however, that if consideration of any and every concept and issue discussed in the previous pages is glossed over or dismissed, curricular planning is placed in peril. These are real concerns affecting the performance of both instructors and students.

Chapter 13

DESIGNING THE EVALUATION
OF STUDENT PERFORMANCE

The purposes and basic theory of the evaluation of student performance have been set out in the first section of Chapter 7. The reader may wish to review them before continuing with the current chapter, in which those same concepts are employed to develop a programme for evaluating the degree of student achievement of curricular and course objectives.

Designing programmes of evaluation is an endeavour of the same complexity as designing programmes of instruction, but with one great advantage. Since evaluation is based on instructional objectives, and since the design of evaluation is not started until the design of instruction is nearing completion, the task of deriving instructional objectives will already have been accomplished and will not need to be undertaken anew. A second advantage is that in the majority of programmes the time that has to be scheduled for administering examinations is considerably less than that set aside for providing instruction, often approaching a ratio of 1:20 to 1:30 in the programme schedule; that is, one hour of evaluation for every 20 to 30 hours of instruction. In spite of these considerable advantages, planning time for evaluation is about the same as that for instruction. Why, then, does the design of evaluation absorb so much time and effort? A description of the steps to be taken in working out a design for evaluation gives a strong indication of the reasons.

Initial Steps

We have already seen that, while faculty and students tend to think of the total curriculum in terms of courses, the development and collection of curricular objectives were carried out prior to the determination of courses. Different, but in some manner related, objectives were then assembled into course packages, which formed the basis of the instructional blueprint. These same objectives, and this same assemblage into course packages, can most easily provide the mode of organization for the evaluation of student performance.

Statements of programme and course objectives are now re-examined in order to determine which of them shall be emphasized in assessment of student performance. Some may be emphasized because they are *Determination* widespread through the curriculum, others because they *of emphasis* represent knowledge, skills or attitudes that must be attained by the students as early as possible in the curriculum on the grounds that their attainment to a satisfactory level is prerequisite to so much that is to be learned subsequently.

With regard to certain other objectives, it may at first be considered unnecessary to assess student attainment of them. For example, some objectives may form necessary though not sufficient precursors of others, so that *Importance* attainment of the latter is a guarantee that the former *of subsidiary* have also been achieved. However, if it happens that a *objectives* student fails to attain the more comprehensive objectives it becomes important to find out whether this is attributable to simple lack of knowledge or whether the student is incapable of applying what he already knows.

In the realm of attitudes and values it becomes important to find out whether, for instance, a student's evident discomfort in working with an unco-operative client results from the client's lack of co-operation or whether the student is not even comfortable when attempting the same transaction with a fully co-operative client. The importance of the subsidiary objectives in evaluation is now apparent, for it is only by assessing the student's attainment of these, in addition to the more comprehensive objectives, that the reason for inadequate performance can be determined and a suitable remedial programme instituted.

A decision has to be made at this time on whether the evaluation programme shall be norm-referenced or criterion-referenced. Norm-referenced testing is based on the assumption that from year to year the classes of students progressing through the curriculum are of approximately equal aptitude. Given that assumption, it is possible to define those students who are unsatisfactory in a course or programme as those constituting the bottom X per cent of the class in the examination results. The choice of a

Norm-referenced evaluation

particular value for X is entirely arbitrary. It is usually defended on empirical grounds: that in several previous years, taken as the norm, X per cent of each class were unsuccessful in this or an equivalent examination. It is also defended on the grounds that competition between students, resulting from a general desire to avoid inclusion in that X per cent, is a beneficial feature of programmes of evaluation, as it parallels competition in the "real world" which students will shortly enter.

Many specialty and licensing boards and some professional schools still adhere to this practice of *normative* scoring on tests, although they have recently seemed to recognize that the fundamental assumption underlying this practice is unwarranted. Some schools and specialty boards are now turning instead to criterion-referenced evaluation based on the opposite assumption that classes can, and do indeed, differ in ability from year to year; in which case it is preferable to define *a priori* the performance that shall constitute the minimum level of competence that is acceptable (referred to hereafter as the *minimum competence level*).

The minimum competence level is determined by a panel of faculty members who are familiar with the expectations of faculty in general in regard to student competence, although their decisions remain subject to

Criterion-referenced evaluation

review by the Curriculum Committee. That level must be determined for every single testing procedure that is used throughout the curriculum, whether requiring an answer to a written question, the performance of a skill, or other response (see the following section for some of the possibilities). In a particular assessment the conglomerate score representing the minimum competence level for that assessment is arrived at most simply by summing the minimum competence levels for the individual test items; the weighting of individual test items is a refinement. Any and all students who perform at or above that pre-defined level will progress to the next portion of the curriculum. For further discussion of these concepts the reader is referred to any standard text on test construction or student assessment (see Ebel 1979).

As with statements of objectives, so with statements of minimum competence levels: these should be stated not only in terms of knowledge acquired but also in terms of skills attained or improved and of attitudes and values adopted.

Models and Criteria

The design of the evaluation programme then turns to available models of assessment, to the types of testing procedures that have proven of use in measuring the attainment of specific kinds of objectives.

Models of Assessment

There are the so-called paper-and-pencil tests: multiple-choice items containing a list of optional answers, short answer questions requiring a sentence or two in response, essay questions that oblige the student not only to supply a (usually) lengthy answer to each question but also to organize that answer into a coherent statement or argument.

In medicine there are patient management problems still in use (see Mc-Guire et al. 1976) which require the student to offer some level of diagnosis and to suggest a preferred treatment. There are simulated patients who present with problems that the student must work through in coming to a plan of management. For measurement of the attainment of skills there are objective clinical exercises in which the student demonstrates a particular clinical skill or medical procedure, makes a decision on the interpretation of medical information, or formulates the next step in a chain of diagnostic or therapeutic procedures. Oral examinations require the student to maintain a dialogue with the examiner(s), allowing the latter to discover the depth of knowledge that the student possesses of a particular topic or of the patient's condition. For consistent measurement of attitudes and values it is possible to use peer review of a student's performance on the wards or in physicians' offices. For all these methods of obtaining information on the attainment by medical students of particular objectives there are parallel methods of particular value to faculties of nursing, law, management, and the various branches of engineering.

To tie into the content of Chapter 7, these assessment methods require the faculty to take a suitable sample of the student's performance, having selected a device that provides evidence of the student's proficiency, and then to measure the sample performance against some standard of attainment of the specific objective.

Criteria for Assessment Models to Meet

Whatever procedures or devices are chosen to assess student performance they must meet certain criteria. These, for the sake of clarity and simplicity, will be discussed in terms of a written test composed of a number of individual questions.

The criteria then are:

1. Validity

An assessment device is valid only when it measures what it is supposed to measure. It then not only provides a score symbolizing the level of performance of the student on the device, it also allows us to infer a similar level of performance by the student over the universe of subject matter sampled by the device. For example, if the minimum competence level demanded of a student is a score of 68 per cent on a test, and the test is a valid one, then we can expect a student who obtains a score of 82 per cent to be capable of demonstrating more than the minimum competence level in *any* test sampling the complete set of objectives. To put such faith in the interpretation of a score we must have some assurance that the test has indeed measured what it was supposed to measure. This assurance can be gained if we obtain positive answers to the following questions about the test:

(a) Does the test adequately sample the content area over which the test is designed to range, and does it sample the situations in which the students are expected to perform? If so, the test is considered to have high *content validity*. For example, a test of the ability to manage elderly arthritic patients would exhibit content validity if it sampled broadly both from knowledge of arthritic diseases affecting the elderly and from a spectrum of elderly arthritic patients, each with particular needs, expectations and problems.

(b) Does the test require the student to give evidence of having attained the educational objectives of the course? If so, then the test is *valid in terms of educational objectives*.

(c) Are differences in performance on the test indicative of differences in later professional performance? If the answer is affirmative, then the test is said to have high *predictive validity*. An example would be a student obtaining a high score on a test of ability to interpret electrocardiograms and later, on duty in a hospital, demonstrating considerable ability in interpreting electrocardiograms correctly.

Validity, however, resides in more than the test; it also resides in the use of the test. Thus, an assessment procedure used with a second-year group of students, when the behaviour and content that it samples lie within the third year of the programme, is obviously an invalid assessment procedure. It is also invalid to test students on the acquisition of essential knowledge or skills which only a graduate professional would be expected to know or have.

For a detailed discussion of issues raised in this section, see Cronbach 1971.

2. Reliability

An assessment procedure or device is reliable if it measures the performance of students consistently. For tests containing several items or questions consistency is measured in two ways. The first way is by correlating the score obtained on one half of a test with the score obtained on the other half of the same test by the same group of students. The halves may be obtained by taking the odd-numbered items to constitute one of the halves and the even-numbered items to constitute the other half. Alternatively the consecutive items making up the first half of the test and those forming the second half may be used. This correlation of half-test scores measures *internal consistency*. The second way of measuring consistency is by giving the same test to the same group of students twice within an interval of several days and then correlating those scores. This correlation measures *test-retest consistency*.

3. Objectivity

The assessment procedure should produce information that is as free as possible of bias introduced by the examiner. Obviously multiple-choice items meet this criterion most effectively, although essay questions need not be discarded because of their inevitable subjectivity. The primary defence against that subjectivity is to provide a plan for scoring essay questions that allots part-marks for specific portions of the required answer, and to ensure that the person who marks the question follows the scoring plan closely and consistently.

4. Feasibility

It is often possible to design assessment procedures that are valid and reliable, even objective, but so costly in materials, in personnel or in time that they are not practical to implement. There is a constant compromise between what is desirable and what is possible, with the quality of the evidence provided by the assessment procedure as the final dimension of judgement

Later Steps

Once the above criteria have been applied in the design of the assessment procedures or devices, attention must be paid to other aspects. The *timing* of the administration of the various tests has to be carefully planned so that the evaluation programme does not get ahead of the instructional programme, thereby requiring the students to demonstrate their learning before they have had the opportunity to learn! There should not be too many tests/examinations close together in time, as fatigue and anxiety might then distort student performance. The planners should therefore determine the proposed *frequency* of evaluation with due care.

A further consideration is the *scope* of the evaluation procedures: there is some danger in trying to evaluate too much at any one time. While there is much to be said for comprehensive examinations, they should not have the total programme as their scope unless they are most carefully designed to evaluate comprehension of basic principles and ability to apply these in various ways, rather than to demand recall of the many minutiae of an entire programme. Finally, a word about *sequence* is apposite. As the instructional programme is intended to provide for an increasing understanding and integration of the learning over time, so the evaluation programme should concomitantly require the student to demonstrate a corresponding development in performance.

Components of the Blueprint

The final product of all these considerations is a design or blueprint for an evaluation programme. It will contain the following:

1. A statement of the purposes of the programme.

2. A complete set of weighted objectives together with a description of the minimum competence level for each.

3. A list of assessment procedures appropriate to these objectives.

4. A basis for the frequency and timing of assessment sessions throughout the educational programme.

5. A statement of the forms of reporting evaluation results to staff and students.

6. Provision for feedback to appropriate persons.

Provision for Appeal

There should also be provision for appeals against an evaluation procedure. The appeal by students is meant in two senses. In one sense, there should be some mechanism allowing students to challenge a particular item on a test either as not being related to the objectives forming the subject matter of that test or as being faulty in design. It may be faulty in design because its meaning is ambiguous, its statements are incorrect or the published answer is incorrect. In the other sense, there must be a mechanism permitting those students who believe that they have been treated erroneously or unfairly by the evaluation system to appeal against the verdict of the system on their performance and to ask for a remeasurement of their performance or another opportunity for evaluation.

As well as appeal by students there should also be an opportunity for appeal by faculty members who consider the evaluation processes inappropriate to the course objectives or to the students at their current level of development.

Chapter 14

IMPLEMENTING THE EVALUATION
OF STUDENT PERFORMANCE

With the design for the evaluation of student performance completed, the task of implementing the blueprint for assessment begins. Just as it was found earlier that certain objectives lend themselves to collection into particular units of instruction, so those same objectives can, and usually should, be grouped into similar units for the purpose of assessment of student performance.

Overcoming Course Constraints

To many, however, this course-based evaluation will suggest that the organization of the instructional programme is too influential in the organization of the evaluation programme. In particular, they *Problems* will argue that there must be objectives transcending the *with* boundaries of any single course. Such is always the *evaluation by* case, but the fact that the primary organization follows *course* course divisions does not preclude the use of assessment procedures that cut across course structure and, indeed, may require the integration of learning from several courses.

Among other matters raised by the emphasis on course structure are the importance of assessing the degree to which students retain what they learn from one course to another, and the need to measure the extent to which students develop not only their understanding of concepts but also their ability to apply these concepts to increasingly complicated professional problems in increasingly complex settings.

As a consequence of these considerations faculty frequently develop assessment procedures intended to provide information on the ability of students to integrate knowledge across course boundaries. The most common

Devices bridging courses

device used to measure the attainment of such integration is the comprehensive examination, administered toward the end of any of the academic years in the programme. An alternative device is the dedication of special days, distributed throughout the curriculum, to the assessment of those skills which become more extensive and complex as students progress through the curriculum. The development of skills of advocacy in law, skills of patient assessment in nursing, clinical skills in medicine, all lend themselves to this periodic form of increasingly demanding assessment. It is the task of the faculty to make certain that this periodic testing occurs as part of an overall plan for the progressive evaluation of professional skills as they evolve.

When special "integrative" courses are inserted into the curriculum in an attempt to counter the compartmentalization of teaching and learning, the integrative ability of students may be evaluated by means of a formal assessment or, perhaps better, by some kind of ongoing evaluation throughout this course.

Apportioning the Work

Although a single group of faculty might possibly develop the total evaluation programme, the scope of the process of test development for the entire curriculum generally precludes any single group from carrying out the task. Accordingly, derivative groups are established by the Curriculum Committee to construct evaluation procedures for individual components of the curriculum.

The terms of reference set by the Curriculum Committee for each group will likely include:

1. To determine which objectives are to be tested. Obviously not all curricular objectives can be tested at any particular time, so that priority is given to those that are more fundamental or more pervasive through the curriculum.

2. To select appropriate methods of assessment for testing the degree of attainment by students of each objective.

3. To establish the minimum competence level for each item in a test and for the entire test.

4. To establish optimal conditions for the assessment procedures. This requires that specific times be set aside for some or most assessment activities. It also requires that the order of assessment of certain objectives be recognized and adhered to, since the attainment of some objectives is dependent on the prior attainment of others.

5. To identify the resources required for tests and other assessment procedures. Resources include clients or patients (real and simulated), observers, space, recording materials such as paper and pencils or videotape cameras and recorders, and reproductions of such materials as company profiles, records of court proceedings or case files, patient records, x-rays or electrocardiograms.

6. To assign to appropriate members of the faculty or administration the task of administering the evaluation programme. This includes giving out and collecting test papers; scheduling patients; hand-marking short-answer and essay questions; collating and summarizing information on class achievement derived from analysis of class performance on individual test items, entire tests and other assessment instruments; measuring class and individual performance against preset standards of minimum competence; and reporting back on individual or class performance to students, interested course instructors and administrators, as appropriate.

7. To provide information to course subcommittees on the performance of students by class, and to formulate recommendations based on that information for the improvement of the curriculum or of student performance. This point will be expanded in the next chapter.

Developing a Structure of Implementation

In order for each derivative evaluation group to function optimally in implementing its programme of evaluation, an executive structure or organization is established. One person is identified as chief administrator of the whole evaluation programme, to whom all others engaged in its implementation are responsible. This person, if not himself the chief executive of the education programme (such as the Associate Dean for Education in the school), is directly responsible to him.

Areas of responsibility of the derivative groups for implementation are clearly delineated so that there are no duplications of, or gaps in, effort. Areas of authority are also defined since, in the process of constructing assessment instruments, small groups often discover each other's territory as a natural link to their own for purposes of assessment. The process known as poaching is then liable to develop. To prevent or minimize its consequences an arena, such as a subcommittee on student evaluation, is specified in which any disputes that arise can be discussed and settled. This implies that channels of communication between the various groups currently planning evaluations are kept open, as are those between each individual group and the chief administrator of the evaluation programme, so that issues and problems can be identified, shared and collectively solved. Finally, the groups provide a schedule of evaluation that is compatible with the schedule of instruction and is sanctioned by the Curriculum Committee.

Providing Support and Encouragement

In all of this work of planning and providing evaluation procedures the derivative groups are given the support and encouragement of the senior group responsible for development and implementation of the evaluation programme. The comments on this topic in Chapter 12 are applicable here as well.

A Sense of Respect

It is worth mentioning that the programme of evaluation of student performance sets the tone of the educational programme of the whole professional school. In spite of generous and detailed descriptions of course intents and objectives it is the programme of evaluation that gives to students what they consider to be the most accurate message of what is, and what is not, important in the professional curriculum. Much stock is placed on getting to know what the faculty expect of students who are taking tests or completing assignments or performing in other evaluation situations.

Students may well, because of their abilities and perseverance, survive an indifferent instructional programme if curricular and course objectives are clear, but they cannot come to terms with an indifferent or invalid system of evaluating student achievement. This, when it exists, is seen by students as an inexcusable default by faculty on their obligation to provide students with assistance in their learning. They soon lose respect for the faculty members they consider responsible, believing that these faculty members have so little consideration for students that they will not take the trouble to mount an evaluation programme meeting even minimum criteria.

Any faculty member who has lived through such a situation in an institution of higher learning knows how long it takes, in spite of honest attempts at remedying the situation, to get the evaluation system working properly once more and so regain for the faculty the respect and trust of the student body. Thus the evaluation programme must give clear evidence of regard for the objectives of the programme, for the students in the programme, and for those faculty who help students individually to accomplish those objectives. Students and faculty members are accountable to each other for their actions, and this requires integrity of purpose and of execution by both parties.

Renewal of Faculty Role

While students move through the curriculum, facing ever new challenges in new situations, faculty members assigned to specific evaluation tasks are uneasy about being caught forever in a particular role. This role is as intellectually demanding as participating in the instructional programme but, unfortunately, there is little glamour associated with all the effort. The system is complex, and every faculty member must spend a certain amount of time learning how to do his job in evaluating student performance.

Attendance at training sessions and workshops is often required, at which both old and new techniques of assessment are examined, studied and refined. It is not unusual for a faculty member to take a year to become effective in his evaluation role and feel comfortable with it. For these reasons the system seems reluctant to replace a contributing faculty member after he has become an evaluation expert. Nevertheless there must be some relief; new members of the faculty have to learn the system, assume responsibility, and be allowed an opportunity to infuse the system with fresh ideas.

A good rough rule seems to be the assignment of a faculty member to a particular role in evaluation for a period of three years at most, with provision for this period to be abbreviated if he should turn out to be quite unsuited to the responsibilities. This means that those in administrative positions need to keep a running list of faculty members ready and willing to begin participating in the programme of student evaluation. They should also be prepared to provide those involved in the programme with the rewards of reporting on research and development in student evaluation at national and international meetings. At these conferences faculty and students share concerns and issues with people from other institutions. They experience and discuss new ideas so that on their return they are better equipped and more inclined to help create new evaluation programmes in their own institutions.

Chapter 15

DESIGNING PROGRAMME EVALUATION

Why Programme Evaluation?

Previous chapters have indicated the time and effort that must be expended by faculty in planning and implementing an educational programme. Yet no matter how much time and effort have been involved, and despite a general acceptance of the programme by faculty and students, once it has been put into operation there will inevitably emerge many ideas of why, when, and how, the curriculum should be modified.

The purpose of such ideas is, in general, to make the curriculum more effective in helping students attain the objectives of the programme, more efficient in the use of resources, and more acceptable to succeeding groups
Improve of students and staff. In order to ensure that ideas of-
the curriculum fered for improvement from time to time are not lost, and that revisions, when undertaken, are based on information that is as reliable as possible, systematic reviews of the curriculum should be planned and undertaken. Reviews should follow an agreed protocol having as its basis the current version, or perhaps a newly amended version, of those statements of institutional goals and educational objectives which the faculty used in designing the current programme. For excellent discussions of the issues involved in designing complex programme evaluations see Cronbach (1983) and Guba and Lincoln (1982).

Review of the curriculum or any part of it serves several purposes in
Show the addition to those mentioned above. For one, it
system demonstrates to individuals and groups having concerns
is open and suggestions about the programme that their ideas are welcome and will be seriously pursued. Thus the system

is shown to be open, with the strength to examine itself and to benefit from that exercise.

In addition, it provides to those who plan and implement the curriculum an evaluation of their work based on criteria they themselves have determined or endorsed. This information has been referred to in Chapter 7 as *Provide internal feedback* feedback. As an example of the use of internal criteria, let us suppose that a group of instructors decided to change the methods of instruction for a particular part of a course by developing a detailed study guide and by placing more responsibility than formerly upon the students for their own instruction. After at least one class of students has completed the modified course the instructors will wish to review this segment of the curriculum in order to determine whether, as a consequence of the use of the new instructional methods, there has been any improvement in the degree or rate of learning. The criterion for determining the degree of learning is student achievement of the course objectives, which the instructors used in setting up their original teaching and then in modifying it.

The instructors may also want to assess the additional cost of the revision in relation to any educational benefit obtained. Cost includes not only the extra funding directly involved, such as that for printing the new study guides and for purchasing extra self-instructional materials, but also the indirect costs such as the diversion to the modified programme of resources like faculty time, secretarial assistance and perhaps student time, at the expense of other parts of the academic programme and possibly at the expense of other activities. By these methods, using internal criteria only, the instructors are able to evaluate their efforts at improving instruction.

A further purpose served by curricular review is that it supplies information, for the benefit of administrators and other interested persons, on the degree to which the programme meets certain external expectations. *Provide data for external assessment* These may have to do with such matters as general features of the curriculum; student/faculty ratios; maximum allotment of students permitted in each clinical setting; access to other clinical and practical settings; administrative procedures; library facilities; and a comparison of student performance locally with overall performance nationally. As an example of the use of external criteria we can take the periodic evaluation by a national professional body of the extent to which its expectations of the professional school's curriculum have been met. This is usually referred to as the process of accreditation. The understanding here is that accreditation of the programme is based almost entirely on the application of criteria that have been determined externally.

What is to be Evaluated

At one time or another the evaluation process is applied to all those aspects of the programme which have been delineated in preceding chapters. One of them is the context in which the curriculum is set. When many years

Context   have passed since the current programme was established it is fair to question the continuing appropriateness of the earlier ideas held by society in general, and by members of the profession, concerning the place of the professional school in the general scheme of things and concerning the role expected to be played by its graduates. Within the parent post-secondary institution, what does its central administration now expect of the programme, and to what extent are those expectations being met?

A second aspect to be studied is the curricular plan or blueprint that was worked out in response to the sets of objectives either generated by the faculty in the initial phase of development or, in an older school, available

Blueprint   in their most recent modification. While it would be counter-productive to review the basic design of a curriculum at short intervals, the blueprint may with advantage be subjected to frequent critical examination. The blueprint is judged by the extent to which it is consonant with the educational goals of the institution and by the extent to which it gives expression to the educational principles adopted by the faculty.

The curriculum itself is reviewed, this involving the distribution of time, space and resources, with the latter including materials, equipment and personnel. The curriculum is then the attempt to follow the blueprint,

Implementation   an account of all those events which took place whether planned or not, with all the successes, blunders, substitutions, improvisations, omissions and serendipitous events, the tale of what happened to the plan when it bumped into reality. The curriculum is judged partly by the extent to which it followed the blueprint and partly by the quality of the curricular outcomes described below.

Sometimes overlooked are the immediate outcomes of the curriculum, except for the mix of successes and failures of the student body as graduates

Outcomes: or as dropouts of the programme. Those who graduate
(1) The   are considered to have altered their behaviour in the re-
students   quired manner and direction, and to be professionally competent, as a direct consequence of their participation in the programme.

A less obvious outcome is a change in those faculty who, as a result of becoming involved in the development and implementation of the programme, have themselves developed new skills, adopted new attitudes, and discovered new talents among themselves. In this sense they, too, are

(2) The faculty   graduates of the programme. Some would have us believe that these enrichments of faculty are found only in a new school with new faculty. On the contrary they can, and frequently do, happen in established schools with interested faculty.

A further outcome is the set of programme materials that evolves with the curriculum. It includes accounts and discussions of the philosophy of the programme and its goals, statements of the principles that are to be used

(3) The programme materials   and their anticipated effects, and study guides developed by faculty for the different courses. These materials are eagerly sought by other institutions having similar goals. Initially they may be sought just out of curiosity but subsequently the ideas contained in them are experimented with, and sometimes copied, by those other institutions. By the sharing of such materials new ideas are disseminated in a most rapid and marketable form, for larger impact. An illustration from law is the development in the early 1980s of the Professional Legal Training Programme by the Continuing Legal Education Society of British Columbia, Canada. This resulted in a series of papers on the purpose and rationale of post-LL.B. professional training, and the circulation of materials related to planning, teaching and evaluation of student performance in Continuing Legal Education during the first years of practice. An illustration from medicine is the set of working papers developed over the 1970s and 1980s by the Faculty of Medicine at the University of Newcastle in New South Wales, Australia. The international distribution of three volumes of their working papers produced an astounding circulation of correspondence on educational goals, the organization of medical school curricula, and faculty development in innovative institutions.

Yet another outcome of the curriculum is the collection of instructional and assessment techniques developed by the faculty in order that the new curricular materials be of maximum benefit to the students. To take an ex-

(4) Techniques of instruction & assessment   ample of instructional techniques, with the increasing interest in the teaching of interviewing, there has appeared a collection of videotapes that can be used both in teaching students the skills of interviewing and in training faculty to become proficient in instructing in those techniques. As an example of assessment techniques, the University of Calgary Faculty of Medicine has developed an integrative examination based on clinical simulations that test application of knowledge and progressive generation of hypotheses as increasing information is obtained.

All of these aspects of the curriculum, that is, context, planning, implementation, and evaluation of outcomes, are studied at one time or another in a regular programme review. Several different models of evaluation programme are available; the interested reader is best advised to peruse Madaus et al.(1983), a book that offers several conceptual models for use by the practitioner. As noted earlier, the model used in this handbook is derived from that of Stufflebeam (in Madaus etal. 1983).

We shall first turn to the evaluation of a course as part of a curriculum and then examine the process of evaluating a whole curriculum.

Methods of Reviewing a Course

Let us assume that a group of faculty and students has been established to review a course. The group will conduct the review sequentially, one step at a time.

Generate Questions

As a first step, broad questions to be asked of the course are generated by the canvassing of faculty members and students. Their submissions generate such questions as: How wisely was the time allotted to the course used in helping students attain the objectives? What were the students' reactions to the course as last presented, and what did they see as being in greatest need of revision? Is the course aimed at too low or too high a level, in comparison with the readiness and motivation of the students and the goals of the whole programme? How well did the last student class attain the course objectives? To what extent were the methods of assessment appropriate to the course objectives? Seldom are questions of context raised in such reviews, these matters being left to a longer, more complex and more formal review of the total curriculum.

Identify Sources of Information

As the second step, the sources of information required to answer these questions are identified. Possible sources include the set of course planning and instructional documents, the comments of students who have just completed the course, analyses of class performance on assignments and examinations, comments and suggestions of faculty members who taught the course. Initial collection and storage of the data are generally the responsibility of some central agency of the Faculty. It may be the group in charge of administering assessments of student performance, or perhaps a dean's office or an office of medical education which has comparatively easy access to records and can best obtain the co-operation of students in completing questionnaires and reaction sheets.

Extract and Analyse Data

The third step of the review is extraction of the requisite information from the identified sources by selected members of the review panel, and analysis of this information in the light of the questions that have been generated. Each member selected for these tasks is allotted a related group of questions to guide his activities. The panel member reports his sources, findings and analysis to the panel's chairman, who circulates the reports to all members.

Discuss the Results

Next, the review panel interprets the information and analyses received, in order that it may comment on issues, problems, strengths and weaknesses in the course. Often this is a most difficult step, requiring that each individual panel member share his perceptions with other members of the group. It is almost impossible to keep personal bias out of the deliberations but it can be expected that the natural checks and balances of a membership as high as eight to ten will keep the work of the panel moving forward in an acceptable direction.

Publish Recommendations

Finally, the panel publishes its recommendations. These may be of various kinds: to modify or eliminate certain features of the course, to endorse particular features and suggest their adoption by other courses, to modify policy, to add faculty in order to strengthen the course, to provide training for instructors in specific areas of teaching or assessment of students, to appoint a new course chairman and/or committee, or to suggest that faculty re-examine specific educational principles. For each recommendation the review panel identifies the person, group or office that shall receive that particular recommendation in order to deliberate on it and take suitable action.

Refer for Action

It can be seen from the foregoing that a specific recommendation may be intended for the chairman of the course under review, other course chairmen, the Curriculum Committee, the course subcommittee, the Dean, the Office of Medical Education, or the entire faculty by way of its representative bodies. It is the responsibility of the person to whom the report is addressed to make sure that the recommendations of the review panel are referred to the appropriate persons and groups for study and further action, and that approved recommendations are implemented without delay.

Addenda

Mention was made above of criteria that are useful in evaluating a programme or course. The most evident is *effectiveness*, defined as the degree to which the objectives are attained by the students. The second is

Criteria used in reviews

efficiency, defined as the degree to which a discriminating use of resources leads to the smallest possible investment of finances, time, effort, personnel, equipment and facilities while maintaining equivalent learning. The third criterion is *acceptability*, defined as the degree to which the course or programme is seen as a positive contribution to the life and function of the institution by the people involved, namely students, staff and administrators. It must be acceptable not only to its own staff but to individuals and organizations outside the professional school and even outside its parent institution. Defining acceptability in such general terms raises the issue of its relationship to effectiveness and efficiency. The general observation would seem to hold that effectiveness and efficiency are necessary but not sufficient conditions for general acceptability.

Furthermore, these three criteria seem to have a chronological sequence. It is to be expected that, for the sake of credibility, a programme or course will first of all be planned to be as effective as possible in helping students attain the objectives of the course. Once effectiveness has been obtained to a satisfactory level, attention will turn to improving the efficiency of the educational enterprise. As the latter becomes more and more efficient, as well as effective, it will also become increasingly acceptable to individual faculty members as well as to students and administrators.

The review of a course completes one cycle of programme development and initiates another. The information derived from evaluation of the course causes the reviewers to look at the original course objectives and at

Cycle of programme development

the learning experiences that were provided by the faculty for student attainment of those objectives. The result is some change in the course, whether in objectives or planned learning experiences or both, which after further presentation must again be reviewed, and so on. Thus the review process is part of a never ending cycle, or rather an upward spiral, given that faculty are never completely satisfied with their current performance in facilitating learning.

As the process is cyclic, recommendations have to be followed through the system to ensure that they arrive at the right destination and that they *Commitment to* stimulate the people there to take corrective action. *follow* Those who receive recommendations from a review *through* panel should feel a strong sense of obligation to carry them out or to provide substitute recommendations that constitute, in the eyes of the review panel, an improvement over their original suggestions.

Methods of Reviewing a Curriculum

Much of the information required to keep the curriculum improving from year to year will be provided by course reviews. Such improvement will necessarily be judged in relation to the blueprint established for each course by earlier planners, and particularly in relation to the course objectives which formed the basis of that blueprint.

Criteria

At longer intervals, however, perhaps first after five years or so, the curriculum will be evaluated as a whole against criteria extending above and beyond the scope of review of individual courses. Effectiveness, for example, in *course* review refers to the extent to which the course objectives have been met. In *curriculum* review the perspective of effectiveness is not confined to the objectives of a single course but encompasses those of the total curriculum and, beyond them, the curricular goals of the institution. Similarly, the perspective of efficiency encompasses the efficiency of the curriculum as a whole. Acceptability of the curriculum not only involves faculty and students, it also involves interested parties external to the school and outside the parent institution.

Who Should Do It

This major evaluation, using the criteria of overall effectiveness, efficiency and acceptability, raises the possibility of a reorientation of the entire educational programme. It is for this reason best carried out by a special task force set up at a senior administrative level of the professional school, for example the faculty council or the Dean's office.

Organization of the Review

The approach taken by the task force can be organized around specific questions arising from the regular instructional activities of the school and also out of a consideration of its social and professional setting. A set of such questions, applicable to review of a medical curriculum, is presented below.

Question 1: How effective has the curriculum been since its inception, or since the previous review?

The answer to this question is provided, on one level, by an analysis of the performance of recent classes of students in the internal certifying examinations. The standards of performance used are those laid down by the school. The graduates themselves are a source of information on curricular effectiveness in the light of their subsequent experience, and their views may be solicited shortly after graduation and at intervals thereafter. Additional information is supplied by their performance in external examinations such as those conducted by professional licensing bodies, although they use standards different from those of the school.

On another level, curricular effectiveness may be gauged by the degree to which those institutional goals which depend for their attainment principally on the undergraduate programme have been realized. For example, if a goal of a medical school is to produce physicians well trained for entry into the traditional clinical specialties, effectiveness of the curriculum in this regard may be judged by the degree of acceptability of its graduates into the appropriate residency programmes and by appraisal of the performance of these graduates by the heads of their residency programmes. If the principal goal of the school is to produce graduates most of whom will opt for careers in medical research, curricular effectiveness may be assessed from information regarding the initial and subsequent career choices of the graduates.

Question 2: In what ways do the expectations held for graduates of the professional school by society, allied professions, and the profession itself, now differ from those current at the time when the present curriculum was being planned?

The information on which to base answers to this question may be obtained from a number of sources. For a medical curriculum there are the members of the health professions in settings other than the medical school. They have impressions of the graduates of the school and how well they performed in routine health care delivery in comparison to graduates of other schools. The graduates themselves are able to provide perceptions of their own strengths and inadequacies as they moved through graduate clinical training and out into medical practice. Patients can be sampled to determine their current expectations of physicians. The views of governments at appropriate levels, on the role of the medical school in the education of health personnel and in the strengthening of health services, as well as their views on the role of physicians and others in providing health care, are normally available via official policy documents as interpreted by official spokesmen during personal interviews. Once all this information is collected it may be evaluated against the writings of experts in the analysis of contemporary life who have a special interest in the role of the physician and of other health professionals in providing health care.

Question 3: At present, what are the expectations of the institution itself?

Answers to this question are found through a study of the institutional goals currently in force, discussions with key faculty members such as the chairman of the Curriculum Committee, and perusal of the most recent policy documents of the Curriculum Committee and other official bodies. It is to be expected that institutional goals also reflect the expectations placed on the institution from the outside, as noted in the second question, but there are certain goals that assume greater or lesser importance in the minds of the faculty compared with the importance placed on them by society in general. These will need to be identified and any incongruencies with the general expectations of society, or any of its components, resolved. The resolution is most often in favour of the institution itself, since the latter consciously takes on only certain societal goals, leaving other goals to other institutions.

Question 4: What changes are required in the curriculum to produce graduates more in keeping with the trend of expectations?

This single question can be expanded to four, covering the four curricular activities involved: the determination of curricular objectives, the processes of planning and of implementation, and the evaluation of student progress.

Question 4A: What changes are required in curricular objectives?

The first answer to this question is defined by comparing present curricular objectives with the responses to Questions 2 and 3 concerning expectations for the school. The second answer is indicated by the responses to Question 1 concerning effectiveness, as determined for example by the performance of several recent graduating classes on the certifying examinations that form part of the evaluation of students.

Those areas in which the students obviously fell far short of curricular objectives, and for that matter those areas in which the students far exceeded them, demand that the associated curricular objectives be re-examined to determine whether they are still appropriate and, if so, whether their level of expectation is appropriate. Some decisions in this area may be held temporarily in abeyance until it is ascertained whether it was the particular calibre of students or the particular mode of instruction that produced the unexpected level of attainment.

Question 4B: What changes are required in planning?

After necessary revisions have been made in institutional goals and curricular objectives it becomes possible to examine the choice of curricular design or pattern. This is more complicated than might at first be anticipated, since quite often there is no single design that carries the whole curriculum. One design will predominate but it is unrealistic to expect that it will be applicable to all areas of the curriculum. The task force will therefore determine whether the predominant design is consistent with the revised goals and objectives and whether departures from this design in specific areas continue to be justified. For example, it may be necessary to judge whether the predominant design in current use in a medical school appears likely to help or hinder the school in producing graduates who are self-reliant, adept at problem solving, and able to use a holistic approach to the practice of medicine, assuming these to be among the revised institutional goals.

Next, the task force will determine whether the current blueprint, constructed on the basis of the earlier curricular designs and objectives chosen by the school, is appropriate to the new designs and objectives. Those parts of the blueprint which require modification, or perhaps deletion, will have to be identified.

Question 4C: What changes are required in the implementation, given the modified blueprint?

There are two aspects to be considered here. One is concerned simply with initial implementation of new or altered parts of the blueprint. The other is more complex, being concerned with identifying the changes that may be necessary in the implementation of unaltered parts of the blueprint. As regards this second aspect, the necessary information will come from several sources. The records of previous course reviews may be examined to determine if there are patterns of criticism extending over several courses or all courses, indicating that changes in policies, procedures or organization are required. Then there are suggestions, some already on file and others newly solicited, from faculty members and students for improving the total curriculum. In addition, records of the use made of various resources by faculty and students as they progressed through the curriculum may be examined. Gaps in logistic support, if not already apparent, will surface at this time.

Question 4D: What changes are required in evaluation?

Information on this matter is probably best obtained from the group that conducted course-by-course evaluation of the curriculum. Members of this group are among the few people on the staff of the school to have a broad view of the curriculum. They may, for instance, have received information from several areas indicating that certifying evaluations take place too frequently, and learning evaluations not frequently enough. Resentment may be building against overuse of some particular mode of examination such as essays or multiple-choice questions. The number of challenges to examination questions, on the grounds of irrelevance or lack of correspondence to stated objectives, may be too large to be ignored. In several courses the absence or inappropriateness of feedback following evaluation may be documented and require correction.

Question 5: What changes are required in faculty recruitment, or in the use made of faculty in planning and implementing the curriculum and in evaluating the students?

The information required to answer this question will be available from the groups reviewing individual courses, and by solicitation from individual faculty members. Course chairmen are particularly valuable for their insights on needs in faculty recruitment.

Question 6: What changes are required in the teaching materials provided within courses?

This question should be left to the last, since the answers to all previous questions affect the answer to this one. Materials are only an extension of the faculty and of their ideas on how a course is to be taught. Useful sources of information to answer this question include (1) individual faculty members who have used the various materials or who have recommended that the students spend time in individual study of them; (2) course chairmen who have commented on the materials used in their courses; and (3) students who were the primary users of the materials.

Priority of Recommendations for Improvement

Once answers to all the above questions have been provided, the task force reviews its own work briefly so as to put its recommendations for improvement of the curriculum in order of priority. It is likely that the recommendations possess different degrees of specificity and have different ranges of applicability. A useful general principle in deciding priorities is that those recommendations having the most widespread effect are considered to be of the highest priority.

Follow-Up

The recommendations are then made available to general faculty for an expression of their collective view, so that some or all of the recommendations receive formal faculty approval. It now becomes the business of the executive apparatus, that is, the Dean, the Associate Dean (Education), and the course chairmen, to put approved modifications into effect. If these procedures are followed, there is every likelihood that the curriculum of the school will be refreshed and that faculty and students will renew their confidence in the acceptability of the programme and its graduates to the medical profession, to society in general and to their own institution.

Chapter 16

IMPLEMENTING
PROGRAMME EVALUATION

Initiation of Review

The responsibility for initiating reviews lies with the person who will be responsible for implementing the recommendations that will be submitted by the reviewing bodies and approved through the appropriate Faculty procedures. Most typically, in a professional school, this responsibility lies with an associate dean or with the chairman of a curriculum committee. It follows that the reports of reviewing bodies are addressed to this person, from whom appropriate action is then expected.

As mentioned in the previous chapter, the occasions on which the whole programme must be studied are relatively infrequent. Reviews of separate courses, or of total activities occurring during a set period of time such as one semester or a single academic year, are much more frequently undertaken and seem to be most productive if they are conducted yearly or in alternate years. For these, the most common unit available for analysis and evaluation is the course, so we shall turn first to implementation of the review of a single course.

Implementing a Course Review

Selecting the Review Panel

The first duty of the initiator is to appoint a chairman for the reviewing body
Chairman   and then, in consultation with the chairman, select the
                  other members. Whatever the method of selection of

169

general members, it is highly desirable that the chairman be most carefully identified as a member of faculty who is familiar with the goals and objectives of the total programme and who understands the place of the course under review in the total scheme of things.

For reasons noted earlier in this handbook the review panel for a course, regardless of the number of factions with a claim to representation on the panel, should consist of no more than eight to ten people. As to representation, a number of considerations point to the prior claim of course chairmen or their equivalent. One consideration is that course chairmen constitute that group of faculty most affected by policy changes resulting from course reviews. Another is that course chairmen already possess an overview of one complete course and can readily deduce practical implications and consequences of proposed changes. A third consideration is that, when a specific problem concerning a course is identified, at least one of the other course chairmen will probably have faced this same problem already and can offer his experience of how it was managed. Finally, the work of the review panel is educational in itself, for the philosophy of the school and the psychology of learning espoused by most of the faculty are made operational by the choice of course content and learning procedures, so that review of the latter constantly raises many of the most fundamental issues related to the former. Of all those who should benefit directly from this educational experience none is more important than the group of course chairmen, for they have the greatest direct influence on every aspect of their own courses.

Members

For all these reasons the majority of the review panel may well consist of chairmen of other courses prerequisite to, associated with, or subsequent to, the course under review. In this way ideas flow quickly from one year of a programme to another during the process of review. The value of student input is now generally recognized and the review panel should therefore contain one or two student representatives including, particularly, a representative of the class that has most recently completed the course. In the review of those courses which, while emphasizing basic concepts, also include a significant clinical component (either as an integral part or else running in parallel or in series) it may well be valuable for the panel to include representation from a group of practitioners or from other special interest groups. This applies reciprocally in the review of those courses which are mainly clinical or practical in emphasis but include a significant basic component.

The procedures of course review are best explained by describing an example of an actual review.

Illustration of a Course Review

By way of illustration, a review of the musculoskeletal course at the medical school of The University of Calgary will be described.

Background

By way of background, the school has a three-year programme leading to the M.D. degree. During the first two years a little over one third of the curricular time is devoted to a series of inter-disciplinary courses dealing with the body systems. Each of these courses is administered by a small subcommittee, which issues a course document for use by students and instructors alike. The document provides a list of objectives; some assumptions about the abilities of students beginning the course; a guide to course content, the amount of detail provided varying markedly from one course to another; a selected list of available study materials; a timetable of scheduled activities or learning experiences; and often a series of problems, sometimes with model answers and a discussion of some major points raised by these problems. It can be seen from this brief description that the course document can serve as a do-it-yourself guide for students of independent bent, who may then sample the scheduled activities for specific purposes, for example to examine patients or to test comprehension of learned material by joining a small group discussion or a quiz session.

One of these courses, the musculoskeletal, deals with the peripheral mechanisms of normal and disordered movements of the body as effected by such structures as skeletal muscles, bones, joints, and the peripheral parts of the nervous system. The course had originally formed part of a much larger one that included the central nervous system and the special senses. However this proved so unwieldy to administer that after its first presentation it was split into separate musculoskeletal and neuroscience courses. It was agreed at that time that the "neurological boundary" between the courses was to be the spinal cord, even though trespass in both directions was inevitable.

Initiation and Review Panel

The musculoskeletal course was reviewed following its sixth annual presentation; there had been one previous review. The decision to undertake this second review was made by the Curriculum Committee and was referred to the Associate Dean (Education) for action. At that time the Associate Dean was using his advisory committee of (all twelve) course chairmen as a review panel, with the addition of the Director of the Medical Instructional Resources Unit, a representative of the Office of Medical Education, and two student representatives, making a total of sixteen members. As a rule, the chairman of the Curriculum Committee attended meetings of each review panel as well. The Associate Dean selected the chairman of another course subcommittee (the cardiovascular-respiratory) to act as chairman of the musculoskeletal review panel.

Format of the Review

A standard format for analysis of a course, produced by one of the course chairmen with experience in arranging course reviews and tested out in those reviews most recently held, was adopted by the panel. This format identified a number of areas to be investigated, that is, the objectives of the course, the course content, assumptions regarding students beginning the course, the learning experiences, the resources used, and assessment of student performance. These areas were apportioned by the panel chairman among selected members of the review panel as follows:

Dr. A: objectives, assumptions, content
Dr. B: learning experiences
Dr. C: resources
Dr. D: student performance

A time limit of six weeks was set for submission of their reports. During this period the other panel members had the opportunity of studying the course document and the course chairman's report, both of which were circulated to all members of the review panel, and of making such enquiries as they saw fit in preparation for the panel meeting.

Guide to Required Information

Each assigned member, Drs. A-D, now had the task of collecting and analysing information relating to his allotted areas. As a guide to the kind of information that would be most useful to the panel, the document provided a number of questions under each area heading. In his inquiry into objectives, for example, Dr. A was to obtain information that would assist him in answering the following questions: (1) Do the objectives inform the student of all those new competencies expected of him by the end of the course? (2) Are the objectives comprehensible to the student? (3) Do all of them seem capable of achievement by most students within the time and with the resources available? (4) Are they at the right level, too low or too high? (5) Do they seem appropriate? (6) Are there redundancies or omissions? (7) Have the objectives been used by students as their principal guide to learning, and by instructors as their principal guide to teaching?

Sources of Data

For the information to help answer these questions various sources were available to Dr. A. These included the course document, the course chairman's report, replies to the student questionnaire, the procedures for

Data on objectives

assessment of student performance, and the individual instructors. It was expected that, as a course chairman, Dr. A would be aware of these sources and would know where they could be consulted. The student questionnaire, as an example, was normally distributed to the class by the Office of Medical Education, which collected the completed questionnaires, made up a class summary of the responses, and stored both the summary and the individual responses. The class summary was then available in the Office for consultation and, since it did not contain any means of identifying the responses or comments of individual students, it could be circulated.

In constructing his reply to the question concerning usefulness of the objectives, Dr. A consulted the class responses to two specific questions: (1) To what extent did you use the course objectives in guiding your studies? and (2) Could you have achieved the objectives without attending any formally scheduled classes? In addition he consulted the students' written general comments. It should perhaps be added that any one source of information might be consulted by several panel members for different purposes. In the present instance Drs. A, B, C and D all made use of class responses to the student questionnaire, although the set of items selected from it was naturally different for each member.

Dr. C's task related to the resources that were used. These were subdivided in the format document into three sections, with a set of questions for each section. The first section concerned people, including faculty and

Data on resources

other instructors, support staff, and patients. The second dealt with materials, including such items as microscopes and slides, books and journals, prepared videotapes, anatomical and pathological specimens, slide projectors, slide-tape sets, laboratory equipment, demonstrations, and films. The third section concerned space, including interviewing and examining rooms, teaching laboratories, lecture theatres, seminar rooms, the learning resources area and display areas.

To take just one of these sections, that concerning resource materials, the applicable questions were as follows: (1) Were the resource materials appropriate to the objectives they were intended to serve? (2) Were they technically adequate? (3) What proportion of the class used them and to what extent? (4) Were they readily available in sufficient numbers when needed? (5) What were the students' opinions of them? The sources of information appropriate to these questions were the course document, the persons who prepared the resource materials, the staff of the Medical Instructional Resources Unit, the staff of the medical library, class responses to the student questionnaire, and the course instructors.

The Director of the Medical Instructional Resources Unit, a key source of information, was frequently consulted on the preparation of resource materials for all courses. The prepared materials were then stored by the

A key source

Unit and subsequently displayed during the appropriate courses as necessary, in the learning resources area of the Unit or in the teaching laboratories or elsewhere. On request, a log of the use of some particular item was kept. In addition, the Director and his staff maintained spot checks of the use of materials during each course, frequently discussing with the students the appropriateness, quality and other aspects of the materials. Dr. C, therefore, consulted the Director of the Unit as one of the principal sources of information regarding materials for the course.

The learning experiences were the task of Dr. B. The questions under this heading were: Is every scheduled activity related to one or more of the objectives? Is the mode of activity appropriate to the objective(s)? For ex-

Data on learning experiences

ample, if the objective is to elicit physical signs, does the scheduled activity involve the student in eliciting the signs himself or does it require him either to watch someone else do it or listen to a lecture on the technique? Where an objective consists of a manual skill such as attempting correctly to feel a spleen, or an application of knowledge such as establishing a differential diagnosis, are all students given sufficient supervised practice during scheduled time? Does each part (or "unit") of a course follow naturally from the previous part and does it lead smoothly to the next one? Is there a unifying theme that applies to all parts and, if so, is this evident to the student? To what extent did the actual learning experiences follow the plan, and what factors were responsible for the differences?

This last question was a source of some embarrassment at every course review for it was apparent that the information to answer the first part of the question was simply not available. On the one hand, the published timetable of scheduled activities was often not specific enough to inform the reviewer of the precise nature of those intended activities. "Lecture", for instance, might be intended to include a demonstration of patients, or to signify a whole class problem-solving session, or to indicate an account of the latest research findings and their implications for clinical practice. On the other hand, no one had monitored the entire course other than (sometimes) the course chairman or an unknown number of students none of whom was expected to provide either an unbiased view or a documented record. This is a matter which, at the time of writing, has still to receive the attention it deserves.

The course chairman's report is one of the key items in any course review. Whereas the procedures outlined above constitute an organized *Course* search, rather like a "review of systems" in the process *chairman's* of taking a patient's history, the course chairman's *report* report generally identifies specific problems and specific merits of the course, akin to "the patient's symptoms" as interpreted and recorded by the doctor. At the time of this musculoskeletal review there was no standard format for course chairmen's reports, so these varied considerably in style as well as in content. The items they all had in common were numerical information on student-contact hours for each instructor and data on types of learning experiences (full-class lecture, large seminar, and so on, as defined and required by the university administration), plus a brief description of the course as planned.

The report of the musculoskeletal course chairman on this occasion brought up a number of significant issues. One of these was whether to continue to include a specific and largely isolated unit on pain in this course. A second was the continued use of one of the affiliated hospitals instead of the Health Sciences Centre as the venue for another unit of the course. A third was the adequacy or otherwise of the course document in regard both to the objectives and to the content. A fourth concerned differences within the subcommittee regarding the basic philosophy of the course and the desirable balance between clinical and biological approaches to the course. A fifth was the continued existence of this course as an independent entity in the curriculum; the report, indeed, listing the arguments for its abolition and the dispersal of its component units among the other courses.

Panel Reports Circulated

The reports prepared separately by Drs. A, B, C and D on their allotted areas were circulated to all members of the review panel, together with the summary of student responses to the questionnaire. As mentioned above, the course document and the course chairman's report were previously circulated. Shortly thereafter the review panel held its meeting.

Panel Discussion and Recommendations

At the review meeting the authors of the reports, including the course chairman, were invited to comment briefly on their reports. A general discussion followed, soon focussing on a number of specific issues. Decisions were reached by consensus in almost all cases, otherwise by majority vote. The review chairman included these decisions, in the form of recommendations, in a letter addressed to the Associate Dean (Education) summarizing the review. The recommendations were as follows:

One: The entire unit on pain, together with its objectives and time allotment, should be transferred out of this course to another place in the curriculum. [The recommendation was forwarded by the Associate Dean to the Curriculum Committee for its decision].

Two: The lack of any independent monitoring of the learning sessions should be drawn to the attention of the Curriculum Committee. [This also was forwarded to the Curriculum Committee].

Three: There should be more consultation with instructors to ensure that teaching schedules for individual instructors are so arranged as not to clash with meetings of professional societies and associations which those instructors feel obligated to attend for purposes of professional development.

Four: There were deficiencies in the course document in regard to objectives and content but revision of the document should await the pending issue of general guidelines by the Curriculum Committee on a standard format for course documents.

Five: As the examination question-bank had too few contributors, greater efforts in this area will be required of the general body of course instructors.

   [Recommendations 3, 4 and 5 were forwarded to the course chairman].

Six: Despite suggestions that the course be discontinued and its component units distributed among the other courses, the musculoskeletal course should be continued as a single block.

Seven: Reconstitution of the subcommittee should be seriously considered as a means of resolving the problems being experienced by that subcommittee. [The suggestion was forwarded to the Curriculum Committee].

Action

The Curriculum Committee transferred the unit on pain to another course and retained the musculoskeletal course otherwise intact. The course chairman, following successful application for sabbatical leave, resigned from the subcommittee. The Curriculum Committee appointed a new course chairman, and minor changes in the course subcommittee recommended by its new chairman were approved by the Curriculum Committee. The following year there were no scheduling difficulties with instructors. Thus, in most respects, the feedback loop was closed, review of the course being followed by changes in the organization and presentation of the course.

Implementing Review of a Curriculum

The task of total curriculum review requires the same attention to strong leadership by a senior member of the faculty, a supervising group of faculty and students, and delegation of tasks of data analysis and synthesis to individuals and groups responsible to the supervising committee, as detailed in our example of a course review.

An illustration of a complete curriculum review, following the pattern described earlier in this chapter, would be so voluminous as to require a separate publication in its own right. In addition, total curriculum reviews are often adapted to local conditions, problems and goals. We have therefore taken a deliberate decision to omit a detailed example of the process.

One of the best recent texts in programme evaluation explores different forms of evaluation serving different purposes (Rossi and Freeman 1985). We strongly recommend its systematic approach to the whole field of evaluation research.

Chapter 17

PULLING IT ALL TOGETHER

I

The reader is no doubt familiar with the practice, in written examinations, of tackling the easy questions first because one can finish them quickly and so spend most of the allotted time on the more difficult ones. The casual reader of this book may have been tempted to follow a similar practice, dipping first into those chapters or sections that seem easiest to read, perhaps because they deal with familiar-sounding topics such as course design or kinds of tests.

Such a reader may be forgiven if he begins to feel uneasy after a very few pages, even after several fresh starts. One reason for his unease is that the later chapters, the ones he is likely to sample first, assume a familiarity by the reader with the theoretical concepts set out in the earlier chapters. Most faculty in professional schools, experts in their own specialized fields, have little time to delve into the specialized field of education and may well be unfamiliar with some of these theoretical concepts or have given them little thought. The other reason for unease is that these later chapters dealing with practical matters are sequential. Any given step is likely based on an essential preceding step, and then itself forms a basis for the steps to follow. Dipping into one of these chapters brings the reader into an isolated spot, not knowing how he got there and unsure of where he is going.

Our expectation is that such a reader will be stimulated to refer back to previous chapters as needed by his particular line of sampling, and in this way will build up an overall view of the subject matter. The present chapter is intended to help him in this process. On the other hand the reader with at least some background in educational theory, as also the dedicated learner, will probably go straight through the book, skimming the parts with which he is already familiar. It will be natural for such a reader to examine the theory before going on to the discussion of practice, and to determine for himself, as he goes along, the appropriateness of the theory and of its practical application. For this kind of reader the present chapter is intended to show the thinking that led to the way the book came to be organized.

II

The basic purpose of any curriculum is student learning and it takes, or should take, pride of place in every professional school. We know that learning in professional schools normally requires people (instructors, patients/clients) and physical resources (rooms, equipment, books and journals). Yet the learning takes place not in a vacuum or an ivory tower but within a particular context, which has many facets. This context is discussed early (Chapter 4) because it bears directly on one of the two most important decisions facing curriculum planners: the choice of a particular type of curriculum (latter part of Chapter 10).

A description of the main types of curriculum should properly follow Chapter 4, forming with it the basic theory underlying the choice of curricular pattern. We have instead, for greater clarity, placed the description of curricular patterns at the beginning of Chapter 10 so that it immediately precedes the discussion on choosing a specific pattern. In a sense, then, Chapters 4 and 10 belong together and may profitably be read in sequence.

III

The other of the two major decisions facing curriculum planners is the formulation of curricular purpose, expressed as the definition of the graduating student (Chapter 9). The theory that guides this expression is complex, forming parts of the chapters on the processes of learning, teaching and evaluation (Chapters 5-7). It is possible, therefore, to take these four chapters together, keeping in mind that there is much more in the first three of these chapters than is needed to understand the fourth one.

These two major interlocking decisions are emphasized here because every other educational decision depends on them. Conversely, the absence of clear-cut decisions in these matters will surely bedevil subsequent discussions and will lead to a proliferation of ad hoc decisions that are neither consistent nor defensible.

IV

The concepts involved in the processes of learning and teaching (Chapters 5 & 6) also underlie the design of entire courses and of the teaching units that compose them (Chapter 11). Similarly the concepts involved in the process of evaluation (Chapter 7) are applied both to the design of evaluation of student performance and to the design of programme evaluation (Chapters 13 and 15 respectively).

V

Every curriculum is the better for being well organized both in its planning and in its implementation. Faculty in professional schools may welcome a coherent viewpoint on the rather peripheral matter (to them) of how one organizes something as complicated as an entire curriculum. Most of us tend to do, and then re-arrange under pressure, rather than work out the organizational scheme beforehand.

The theory of organization is dealt with in Chapter 8. It finds application in three areas of implementation: the implementation of course and unit design (Chapter 12); that of evaluation of student performance (Chapter 14); and that of programme evaluation (Chapter 16). These four chapters can be considered a functional unit and therefore be read sequentially.

VI

It can be seen from the foregoing that there are several ways of reading this book, each sequence being appropriate to some readers. A particular reader may find it essential to read parts of it more than once, using a different sequence each time. We concluded that the least confusing way of arranging the topics was to set all the chapters dealing with theory first, following the introductory section, and all the chapters dealing with application of theory afterwards. This, at least, is a sequence well understood by the faculty of professional schools.

VII

If we, the authors, have accomplished our purpose in writing this book we expect that it will be pulled off the shelf frequently and used as orientation by anyone beginning the task of designing, redesigning, implementing or evaluating the curriculum of a professional school. Many are engaged, or are about to engage, in this extremely complex process; and curricular development, like research, is a never-ending process. For success, both require incessantly inquisitive minds.

APPENDIX A

Below is a list of educational objectives in medicine, law, and nursing, illustrative of levels in the Cognitive Domain.

1.00 KNOWLEDGE

  1.10 Knowledge of Specifics

   1.11 Knowledge of Terminology

   Define a non-aligned fracture.

   Define joint tenancy.

   Define the modes of administration of drugs.

   1.12 Knowledge of Specific Facts

   List four common problems of infants of low birth weight.

   Recall that in law a valid consent involves both awareness and assent.

   Recall that widows and widowers are far more susceptible to illness during the year after the death of the spouse than at any other time.

  1.20 Knowledge of Ways and Means of Dealing with Specifics

   1.21 Knowledge of Conventions

   Define movements by reference to the standard anatomical position.

Describe the standard forms used in recording transfer of land titles.

Recall the usual responsibilities assigned to a unit clerk at a nursing station in a hospital.

1.22 Knowledge of Trends and Sequences

Describe the natural history of AIDS.

List recent changes in laws governing taxation of individuals' incomes.

Recall the factors that predispose to intestinal obstruction.

1.23 Knowledge of Classifications and Categories

Present the biochemical classification of the glyco-saminoglycans.

List the types of defences to intentional torts.

List the categories of activities of daily living.

1.24 Knowledge of Criteria

Give the criteria for a diagnosis of rheumatoid arthritis.

Distinguish between legal interviewing and legal coun-selling.

Distinguish among primary, secondary and tertiary sour-ces of nursing information regarding a patient.

1.25 Knowledge of Methodology

Describe how the blood pressure is measured clinically.

Describe the process of obtaining an informed consent to a surgical procedure.

List the steps involved in inserting a Swan-Ganz catheter.

1.30   Knowledge of Universals and Abstractions in a Field

    1.31   Knowledge of Principles and Generalizations

    Recall the pharmacological principles underlying selection of the different routes by which drugs may be administered to patients.

    Recall the principle that in the tort of assault there must be a voluntary act, the mind prompting and directing the act which is complained of.

    Recall that a nurse must identify environmental, physical and psychosocial factors in patient illness.

    1.32   Knowledge of Theories and Structures

    Describe the theories of causation of malignancy.

    Describe the concept of negligence in both its civil and its criminal context.

    Describe the aetiologies of psychosomatic illness.

2.00   COMPREHENSION

2.10   Translation

Express the history, as given by the patient, in the technical terms of a medical history.

Describe to a client the meaning of compensation for "pain and loss".

Translate nutritional requirements into categories of foodstuffs.

2.20   Interpretation

Express in the vernacular a correct description of an element in a plain x-ray film of the chest.

Interpret the ruling of a judge in a civil case to the client who "lost".

Explain to a patient the results of that patient's laboratory tests.

2.30 Extrapolation

Determine the effects of the currently aging population on the costs ten years from now of prescription drugs for Canadian pensioners.

Predict, after studying reports of public hearings on proposed legislation, the revisions likely to be made.

Predict the problems in adjustment of lifestyle and eating habits of an adolescent diabetic.

3.00 APPLICATION

Calculate the dose of Penicillin V required for a four-year-old child with a penicillin-sensitive infection.

Record systematically the pertinent facts of a problem presented by a client seeking legal advice.

Demonstrate to a patient the proper preparation and use of an inhaler providing a measured dose of a drug.

4.00 ANALYSIS

4.10 Analysis of Elements

Distinguish between a patient's complaints and his interpretation of those complaints.

Identify two possible outcomes either of which will suit a client who retains your services in an attempt to alter the conditions of a contract.

Determine, following structural changes in the heart resulting from a myocardial infarction, the consequent physiological alterations.

4.20 Analysis of Relationships

Determine the consistency between a patient's complaints and the results of physical examination and laboratory studies of the same patient.

Identify the ratio decidendi of a case, that is, the material facts of the case plus the decision thereon.

Identify the relationships among the factors involved in developing a plan of treatment for a patient.

4.30   Analysis of Organizational Principles

Recognize the essential elements of a psychiatric assessment of a patient.

Identify what "worked" in negotiating a particular settlement on behalf of a client.

Identify the factors that were considered in recruiting community resources for the family of a child with a severe physical handicap.

5.00   SYNTHESIS

5.10   Production of a Unique Communication

Present a patient before colleagues and instructors.

Formulate the issues in a case to be appealed.

Write a nursing note on the day's progress of a patient in intensive care.

5.20   Production of a Plan or Proposed Set of Operations

Submit a plan to trace the causes of an outbreak of a new disease.

Develop a plan of argument designed to persuade the court of the reasonableness of the defendant's actions.

Develop a nursing plan for a post-operative patient.

5.30   Derivation of a Set of Abstract Relations

Formulate a differential diagnosis, given the history and the results of a physical examination of a patient.

Determine the relationships between facts and issues in a split decision.

Formulate the nursing requirements of a patient who has just been admitted to Emergency following involvement in a motor vehicle accident.

6.00 EVALUATION

6.10 Judgements in terms of Internal Evidence

Evaluate the quality of a case presentation in terms of its clarity, sequence, consistency, and hypotheses concerning aetiology.

Judge an oral argument in terms of its (a) clarity in stating the nature and history of the case, (b) presentation of the facts, (c) clarity in stating the applicable rules of law, (d) ability to provide answers to expected questions from the court.

Evaluate a nursing plan for a patient in terms of clarity, focus, brevity, short- and long-term objectives, and flexibility.

6.20 Judgements in terms of External Criteria

Evaluate a proposed plan of management of a patient in the light of recent publications dealing with the management of similar cases.

Determine the limits of proper professional conduct in a potential conflict of interest.

Evaluate the effects on the nursing profession of a statement on a controversial matter issued by a nursing organization.

APPENDIX B

Below is a list of educational objectives in medicine, law, and nursing, illustrative of levels in the Affective Domain.

1.00 RECEIVING (ATTENDING)

1.1 Awareness

Is aware that a patient is suffering from recent anorexia.

Is aware that justice is not parcelled out equally to all citizens.

Is aware that some types of patients receive more attention from health care workers than do other types.

1.2 Willingness to Receive

Feels comfortable when the consulting physician gives his opinion on a patient referred to the consultant by the student.

Attends carefully when clients relate their problems.

Listens to repeated complaints of patients on the wards.

1.3 Controlled or Selected Attention

Listens carefully when the Emergency Room nurse makes specific suggestions for patient care.

Is alert to observations of peers on the quality of his case presentations.

Pays particular attention when other nursing students in the same clinical setting offer feedback on performance.

2.00   RESPONDING

2.1   Acquiescence in Responding

Complies with aseptic procedures in the Operating Room.

Follows routines in filing small debt claims.

Reviews patient charts with the nurse on the previous shift when coming on ward duty.

2.2   Willingness to Respond

Willing to follow hospital regulations affecting his role as a student physician.

Assumes responsibility for improving his own proficiency in argument.

Speaks with a physician who has complained of the "overfullness" of nursing information in his patients' charts.

2.3   Satisfaction in Response

Takes pleasure in offering a well-researched and well-constructed patient presentation to the attending physician.

Enjoys the challenge of difficult legal problems.

Obtains satisfaction from reassuring patients who are anxious regarding impending surgery.

3.00   VALUING

3.1   Acceptance of a Value

Accepts that for some patients the ultimate goal of current management is not a cure but an accommodation to a chronic condition.

Feels comfortable working as a lawyer even with objectionable clients.

Accepts that for some patients the ultimate goal of current management is not a cure but an accommodation to a chronic condition.

3.2   Preference for a Value

Assumes responsibility for reviewing periodically all charts of patients assigned to him.

Keenly concerned to avoid conflicts of interest.

Assumes responsibility for reporting to visiting family members the progress of a patient recovering from surgery.

3.3   Commitment

Assumes an active role in opposing the institutionalization of elderly patients whose health can be maintained adequately and efficiently by a home care programme.

Maintains that the judicial system can be made more equitable and efficient without the expenditure of extra government funds.

Places the welfare of the patient first in all nursing situations.

4.0   **ORGANIZATION**

4.1   Conceptualization of a Value

Forms judgments as to the responsibility of physicians for conserving public funds assigned to health care programmes.

Identifies the characteristics of an ethical lawyer.

Delineates the characteristics of a caring nurse.

4.2   Organization of a Value System

Uses local standards of health care in determining treatment regardless of the effect on his own remuneration or professional image.

Develops a plan for keeping current on developments in the law in spite of the demands of a busy practice.

Places individual professional goals in the context of the health care team.

5.0   CHARACTERIZATION BY A VALUE OR VALUE COMPLEX

5.1   Generalized Set

Adopts evident and thorough plans of diagnosis and therapy for all patient problems brought to him.

Develops consistent and effective routines for interviewing and counselling clients on legal matters.

Develops and consistently uses criteria for evaluating nursing care plans.

5.2   Characterization

Gives evidence, by his professional behaviour, of the adoption of a strong personal and professional code of ethical practice.

As a family lawyer, consistently promotes mediation first to clients seeking divorce.

Gives clear indication to the patient under stress that as a nurse she is open to any concerns no matter how awkward the issue or situation may seem to the patient.

APPENDIX C

Shown below are learning and teaching procedures appropriate to levels of educational objectives in the Cognitive, Affective, and Psychomotor, Domains.

TYPE OF OBJECTIVE	LEARNING PROCEDURES	TEACHING PROCEDURES
Cognitive Domain		
1. Knowledge: recall and/or recognition	Reading Listening Association of ideas Drill with feedback	Lecture Reading materials Audiotapes Slides, films Mnemonic devices
2. Understanding/ comprehension of ideas	Interplay of minds Association of ideas	Printed materials Charts & diagrams Group discussion Inquiry (questioning) Programmed instruction Lab. demonstration
3. Application of a principle	Identifi- cation of the appropriate principle Using the principle	Directed questioning Assigned exercises (basic or clinical) Lab. exercises (which follow a protocol)

TYPE OF OBJECTIVE	LEARNING PROCEDURES	TEACHING PROCEDURES
4. Problem-solving (analysis, synthesis, evaluation)	Problem-solving (actual or simulated problems)	Demonstration of the process Observation and feedback Role-playing Computer-assisted instruction Gaming

Affective Domain

5. Attitudes, values	Imitation of a professional role model Action as a consequence of personal judgement arising from impact of materials or conditions	Selecting the appropriate role model Selecting materials and conditions and placing in proper setting to make an impact on the learner

Psychomotor Domain

6. Manual or technical skills	Practice	Demonstration Observation of practices with feedback, using video-tape

GLOSSARY

The glossary is in two parts. Part One consists of terms that form part of the technical language of education. Some of these terms, for example assessment, are understood differently in different educational circles so that it is necessary to define the way they are used in this book. Part Two consists of terms that form part of the technical language of medicine. They are included for the use of those who may wish to follow the medical examples scattered throughout the book. Definitions are set aside in favour of explanations in lay terms when the latter are considered more appropriate for the purpose.

Part One

Assessment   The entire process of identifying the performance to be measured, constructing the test to measure the performance, administering the test to the student, and recording the measurement. The result of an assessment is some symbol (either a letter grade or a score), or a checked list of activities observed, or a descriptive term such as "Satisfactory" or "Pass".

Authority   The right to act, or direct others to act, in pursuit of organizational goals, together with the legitimate power to use rewards and penalties for the same purpose. Cf. power.

Bias   A process, occurring at any stage of inference, tending to produce results that depart systematically from the true values.

Blueprint   1. The detailed plan of learning and teaching intended to take place during scheduled hours of a curriculum, a course, or part of a course. It informs students and faculty of what has been arranged for them during those hours, that is, who is to be doing what, when, where and how.

2. A similar plan for evaluation of students against objectives of a curriculum or course.

Cognitive   The cognitive domain includes those objectives which deal with the recall or recognition of knowledge or the development of intellectual abilities and skills.

Concept   A general notion or idea. Perhaps the best-known medical examples are (1) the concept of tiny, unseen organisms being the cause of some diseases, constituting the foundation of microbiology; (2) the concept of self and non-self, constituting the foundation of immunology.

Course chairman   The faculty member who chairs the group responsible for planning and executing a course.

Criterion-referenced (assessment)   A method of determining a candidate's score using predetermined criteria of performance without reference to the score obtained by any other candidate. Cp. norm-referenced.

Curriculum   A focussed series of courses of study or training. It is more than instruction (q.v.).

Derived score   A collection of raw scores (q.v.), e.g. total marks obtained by students in an examination or for an assigned term paper, has a mean value and a standard deviation. When the latter are known, it is possible to use them to convert each of the raw scores to a different "derived" score such that the mean of the derived scores is a selected value and the standard deviation is also a selected value. As an illustration, the raw scores obtained by candidates on the examinations of the *National Board of Medical Examiners of the United States* are converted into scores that arbitrarily have a mean of 500 and a standard deviation of 100. These are derived scores.

Design   The broad features of a curriculum that must be decided before work on the blueprint can be started. These features include optimally an ordered set of objectives, a pattern or patterns of instruction, a list of courses, a time frame, and a statement of the kinds of resources needed.

Elective   Scheduled hours in a curriculum set aside for studies determined by the student. The latter may determine, either alone or in consultation with a faculty member, the objectives of these studies, the learning methods to be used, and the form of evaluation, if any. Alternatively, the student may simply select one or more from a predetermined set of courses, control of which is in the hands of faculty. Whether this second type should be called "elective" is arguable.

Evaluation   The placing of a value on student performance following observation or measurement of that performance. A score of 65 per cent states a measure of performance, the decision "pass" gives the evaluation of that performance. Evaluation implies a judgement based on criteria, explicit or not. "He's not safe to let loose on the public" is an evaluation sometimes made by examiners of medical students and graduates based on criteria that are seldom made explicit. Evaluations may, or may not, be taken to include the assessment (q.v.) that precedes assignment of the value.

Examination   One means of obtaining a measure of student performance. At a set time and set place the student is asked to respond to a series of questions or to demonstrate a number of skills. See Assessment.

Faculty   In this book, "Faculty" with a capital F refers to a Faculty of Medicine, a Faculty of Social Welfare, a Faculty of Law, and so forth; "faculty" with a small f refers to the teaching staff of a university or professional school.

Goal   A broad statement of general purpose. Often such a statement employs value-laden words without indicating criteria for values, for example "To produce good doctors". (What are the criteria for "good" doctors at the time of their graduation?)

Instruction   Activities of teachers designed to facilitate learning by students.

Integrated   A curriculum in which the separate disciplines are not taught separately, so that they cannot even be separated out by examining the schedule of instruction. What is to be studied draws on the disciplines as necessary but only in the context of the problems or situations under study. However, the fact that almost all faculty have received their professional training *in a discipline* makes for difficulty in operating an integrated curriculum. The first task is usually to integrate faculty!

Inter-disciplinary   Studies organized in such a way that concepts, principles and mechanisms of different disciplines can be studied concurrently. Usually faculty members representing the various disciplines teach in teams. Synonym: multi-disciplinary.

Learning   A process producing a consistent change of behaviour in terms of knowledge, skills, interests, attitudes or values.

Learning experience   A scheduled opportunity to learn specific things by participating in specified activites. Some learning experiences in medical schools are: listening to lectures, performing laboratory experiments, observing births, reading, presenting patients to colleagues.

Line and staff   The chain of command in an organization passes along a series of managerial positions successively from superior to subordinate, finally reaching the rank-and-file workers. These positions form the "line"; for example, in a professional school the Dean, associate deans, department heads, and so on.

Assisting the line positions, but not usually forming part of this chain of command, there may be a number of advisory and consultative positions. These form the "staff"; for example the finance officer, an office of professional education, an audio-visual unit, personal and administrative assistants to the Dean.

Master planning group   A group, consisting entirely or largely of faculty members, having the responsibility for planning, operating and modifying the curriculum. The most popular name for such a group in medical schools is Curriculum Committee or Medical Education Committee or some variant of these.

Mechanism   The process or processes by which some structural, functional or developmental change is brought about. Knowledge of a mechanism involves knowledge of which structures perform what actions.

Multi-disciplinary   Synonym: inter-disciplinary.

Multiple choice   A type of examination question in which the student selects the correct answer, the best answer, or a number of correct or appropriate answers, from a list of answers provided.

Norm-referenced (assessment)   A method of describing the performance of a student by comparing his score with the scores of the entire class or of some other reference group. The standard is set by that particular class or reference group, not by criteria or performance levels determined prior to the assessment. Cp. criterion-referenced.

Objective   A statement of those things the learner is expected to be able to do as the result of specific studies, the context in which the doing of those things will be performed and tested, and the degree of competence expected. In higher education it is often a statement of the kinds of things, rather than specific things, that the learner is expected to do. This statement constitutes a *behavioural* objective. A *content* objective states the knowledge, or the categories of subject matter (facts, principles, concepts, relationships), that the student is expected to learn in order to be able to achieve the behavioural objective(s). Cp. goal.

Organizing element   The reiterated theme on which a course, or part of a course, is organized. For the student it provides a common ground for the various parts of the course. For example, in medicine, physical examination as a skill, antigen-antibody relationship in immunology.

Organizing principle   The basis on which a particular *sequence* was selected for the parts of a course. Knowing it, the student can see the natural progression of the course, for example from theory to practice, from normal to abnormal.

Patient management problem   A form of written medical examination, the intent of which is to ascertain the decisions made by a candidate when a patient with a medical problem consults the candidate as physician about this problem. To a large extent the candidate can select the questions he wishes to ask the patient and is then given appropriate responses; he can select the physical and laboratory tests he wants performed and is then given their results; he interprets these results and selects a regime of management. The technique reveals not only the candidate's decisions but their sequence as well. Through this technique the competence of the candidate may be measured in various ways.

Planning   Curricular planning includes (1) constructing a curricular design and (2) making a blueprint. The former describes the kind of curriculum it is going to be, the latter provides the details.

Power   Possession of control over others, legitimately or not. Cf. authority.

Preceptor   A faculty instructor, or one approved to act as a faculty instructor, for an individual student or a small group of students, usually for the duration of a set of studies such as a course or a period of elective study.

Principle   A highly general statement (or "law") admitting of many special applications or exemplified in a multitude of cases.

Programme   The performance as a whole. In professional education it includes such components as the curriculum, the procedures for admission, the conduct of student affairs, and relations with affiliated institutions.

Raw score   The total number of points a candidate scores on an examination may be expressed by this number or as a percentage of the maximum possible number of points. A score of 75 points out of a possible 125 points may be expressed as "75" or as "60 per cent". Cf. derived score.

Reinforcement   Promotion of desired behaviour by rewarding that behaviour and by punishing undesired behaviour. Forms of reward and punishment for adults must be subtle.

"Service" course   A term used by faculty to indicate a course provided in one's discipline or area of specialization for students whose major area of interest lies outside one's own discipline or Faculty or even outside the university.

Simulated patient   A person who acts the part of a patient. The acting may require training, especially if particular physical signs or psychological traits are to be mimicked or if particular physician-patient relationships are involved. Often used in the assessment of students.

Simulation   An exercise in which events and people are pre-programmed, requiring the student to make decisions, then to act on them, and to react to the programmed consequences of the act. The exercise is often a selected sample of activities from real-life situations.

"Soft" sciences   The disciplines and areas of study that deal with the ways in which people behave; for example, psychology, sociology. They have in the past been regarded with considerable suspicion by natural and physical scientists as being in some important ways "inferior" to the "hard" sciences, and less scientific. It was believed that medical students needed only to study the "hard" sciences to grapple successfully with medical problems. The need for students and practitioners to apply an understanding of human behaviour to their medical practice was often acknowledged in word though seldom in deed. Cp. "hard" sciences.

Teaching   Its general meaning of communicating knowledge or skills is well known. Recent emphasis on learning, rather than on teaching, has altered the undertones of the word so that the emphasis is rather on helping the student to learn. For example, creating self-instructional materials can be considered teaching, although the student's interaction with the materials occurs later. Constructing examination questions for the purpose of student learning, rather than evaluation, can be considered teaching. Evaluation of student performance is also teaching, provided feedback is given to the students. Synonym: instructing.

Unit manager   The faculty member who assumes the responsibility for the execution of a part of a course within the framework laid down by the course committee. A unit manager may, but need not, be a member of the course committee.

Part Two

Accreditation   When a country possesses a number of medical schools, the graduates of a school may be granted a licence to practise outside the region containing that school only (a) if regions have reciprocal licensing agreements, or (b) if some national body has certified that the school is meeting national standards, that is, if the school is accredited. Clinical specialty training may be recognized at the national level only if the training programme has been accredited by the appropriate national body.

Apgar score   A number symbolizing the physical condition of a baby very shortly after birth.

Aspergillosis   An illness produced by a fungus of the genus Aspergillus.

Basic (medical) science   The term is impossible to define rigorously. Many medical school curricula are divided into two consecutive parts. The first consists of a number of disciplinary courses such as anatomy and physiology, which are taught mostly in lecture rooms and laboratories; these are the "basic" sciences. The second part consists of disciplinary courses such as internal medicine, surgery, and obstetrics, which are taught mostly at the bedside; these are the "clinical" sciences, for which a knowledge of the basic sciences is said to be prerequisite. Furthermore, some disciplines such as pathology, microbiology, and pharmacology, are difficult to classify, as they are perceived differently in different institutions. Other basic disciplines such as psychology and sociology are slowly coming to be recognized as prerequisite to modern clinical studies.

Biomedical   Pertaining to the natural sciences as applied to medicine. The term is an affectation, for in any given case either "biological" or "medical" is a better word.

Cervical nodes   Cervical refers to position in the neck. Nodes (lymph nodes) are small, discrete masses of special (lymphoid) tissue grouped in strategic positions in the neck and throughout the body. Under certain conditions they enlarge and may be easily felt.

Clerkship   A period of mostly clinical studies, varying from one to three or four years, in which the medical student spends the greater part of his time "at the bedside", that is, attending patients under the supervision of his instructors.

Community hospital   A hospital neither controlled nor funded by the university or medical school but possibly used by the medical school for teaching.

Congenital   Present at birth.

Cranial nerves   Nerves that are attached directly to the brain and concerned with such functions as chewing and swallowing, speaking, moving the eyes, tasting.

Differential diagnosis   A list of disorders that could be responsible for the patient's condition. The list is usually, though not always, presented in order of decreasing probability or decreasing urgency of intervention.

"Hard" sciences   The sciences that deal with material things; the physical and natural sciences, including (sometimes) mathematics. While the practice of medicine is generally accepted as being both an art and a science, those who emphasize the scientific aspect favour study of the "hard" sciences as prerequisite to admission to medical school. Cp. "soft" sciences.

Hiatus hernia   A condition in which, most commonly, part of the stomach lies in the chest and part in the abdomen (instead of the whole stomach in the abdomen).

Humerus   The bone of the upper arm, extending from shoulder to elbow.

Hydramnios   An abnormal condition of the foetus when the volume of "the waters" (amniotic fluid) is excessive.

Incontinence   Inability to control excretory function.

Intern   A physician working in a hospital, usually for one year immediately following graduation, in order to fulfil a prerequisite for licensing or as a preparation for entry into a residency (specialty) programme. The lowest rank of medically qualified personnel in a hospital.

Internist   A physician whose specialty is internal medicine.

Kelvin   A scale of temperature in which "zero" describes an absolute lack of heat (or absolute cold), and a doubling of any reading indicates a doubling of the quantity of heat (per unit). On this scale the freezing point of water is 273° K.

Krebs cycle   A series of chemical reactions occurring in living cells which produces large amounts of energy. Named for Sir Hans Krebs.

Lymphoma   An overgrowth of lymphoid tissue, most often a form of cancer.

Mastectomy   Surgical removal of the breast.

Neoplasm   A growth, whether or not it is cancerous.

Neonatology   A clinical discipline that deals with newborns up to the age of four weeks.

Organic disease   Disease in which abnormal body structure or abnormal product of the body can be demonstrated.

Peripatetic   A form of practical examination in which specimens are displayed serially along benches or tables and each candidate moves from one specimen to the next at specified time intervals, attempting to answer the questions relating to each specimen in turn within the given time-limit.

Phobic neuroses   Emotional disorders involving morbid fears.

Physical signs   Objective evidence about a patient collected in the course of a "physical" examination, in which the doctor uses his unaided senses with no more elaborate instrument than a stethoscope.

Pre-clinical   In traditional medical schools the first years of the curriculum are devoted to a study of the so-called basic medical sciences (q.v.). The later years are devoted mainly to clinical studies. The early courses are lumped together as the pre-clinical studies, and are said to be studied during the pre-clinical years.

Now that clinical and basic sciences are being taught in the same years of the curriculum the term "pre-clinical" is falling into disuse.

Primary care   The type of health care available on first contact of the patient with the health care system. It may, or may not, be provided by physicians. If it is, those physicians are called general practitioners, family physicians, or some such name. In many countries primary care is provided in part by medical specialists, for example by paediatricians, obstetricians or internists.

Prolapse   A falling down of some body structure into an abnormal position; most commonly used to describe a dropped womb.

Resident   A medical graduate in a clinical specialty training programme of several years' duration. (The common clinical specialties are internal medicine, family practice, surgery, psychiatry, obstetrics & gynaecology, paediatrics).

Risk (At risk)   More likely than the rest of the population to acquire, or suffer from, a particular disorder or condition.

Rotating internship   Instead of spending the full period of internship in one clinical discipline, the intern (q.v.) spends short periods of time consecutively in several different disciplines. Each of these periods is called a rotation.

Rounds   A tour of patients in a ward by the doctor in charge of those patients or in charge of the ward, or by a clinical instructor with students ("teaching rounds"). The term has been extended to include a discussion of patients and related clinical matters that takes place near, but not in, a ward; or of patients' records ("chart rounds"); or of specific cases such as those patients who died while in the hospital ("death rounds"). A clinical lecture is sometimes called a "grand round".

Secondary care   Health care provided by medical specialists, usually on referral of the patients by primary care personnel. Some medical specialists in certain countries also provide primary care (q.v.).

Service activities   The care of patients by clinical faculty members which is not concerned with any academic function such as teaching.

Service work   The term applied to hospital ward work of a technical nature, such as taking blood samples from patients or examining samples of urine with a microscope.

Skeletal muscles   The "voluntary" muscles.

Special senses   The senses of sight, hearing, smell, taste, balance.

Sutures   The edge-to-edge joints between the bones forming the greater part of the skull.

Teaching hospital   A hospital, closely associated with a medical school, in which medical students are officially taught. A few such hospitals are controlled by medical schools and are fiscally part of them. Most, however, merely have some form of agreement with the medical school which, for example, requires those who hold certain hospital positions to hold academic appointments as well. Rarely a teaching hospital will admit only those patients considered suitable as teaching subjects. Cp. community hospital.

Tertiary care   That type of health care requiring sophisticated facilities and very highly specialized medical and supporting staff, usually in a large and lavishly equipped hospital. Aside from emergencies, admission to such a facility is normally via referral by a physician.

Tomography   The recording of an X-ray image of a body-slice. The "slice" is an optical section produced by the machinery used. Standard X-rays (radiographs) show larger or smaller whole regions of the body, such as the chest or wrist.

Trochanter   A projecting piece of a normal bone, usually referring to those at the upper end of the thigh bone.

Urinalysis   Examination of the urine in order to determine such properties as its clarity, colour, sugar content.

BIBLIOGRAPHY

American Association of Medical Colleges. 1988. *AAMC Curriculum Directory.* Washington, D.C.: A.A.M.C.
— Published annually, this compendium provides an overview of the current structure of curricula of medical schools in the United States and Canada.

Ausubel, D.P. 1964. Some psychological aspects of the structure of knowledge. In Phi Delta Kappa, *Education and the Structure of Knowlege*, 233-248. Chicago: Rand McNally.
— An illustration of how one psychologist sets the context of learning.

Barrows, H.D. & Tamblyn, R.M. 1980. *Problem-based Learning: An Approach to Medical Education.* New York: Springer.
— An essential volume for the medical educator.

Berelson, B. & Steiner, G. 1964. *Human Behavior: An Inventory of Scientific Findings*, 358. New York: Harcourt, Brace & World.

Bloom, B.S. (Ed.) 1956. *Taxonomy of Educational Objectives: Handbook I: Cognitive Domain.* New York: David McKay.
— A useful classification system for educational objectives. See the sample objectives of Appendix C.

Bloom, B.S., Hastings, J.T. & Madaus, G.F. 1981. *Evaluation to Improve Learning*. New York: McGraw Hill.
— This second edition of a classic in the field is based on the classification systems for educational objectives displayed in Bloom (1956) and Krathwohl *et al.* (1964). A third classification system using objectives in the psychomotor domain is given in Harrow (1972).

Cantor, N. 1953. *The Teaching-Learning process*. New York: Dryden Press.
— Cantor was a university professor of considerable influence on medical education, primarily through his activities with medical educators at the University of Buffalo in the mid 1950s. He was an inspiring teacher and his work provided conceptual underpinnings for the Buffalo Project financed by the Commonwealth Fund, described by Miller (1980).

Caplow, T. 1976. *How to Run any Organization: A Manual of Practical Sociology*. Hinsdale, Ill.: The Dryden Press.
— Preparatory to writing the sections on organizational structure the authors reviewed several texts on organizational structure, management, leadership, and related fields, in general finding them disappointing. We tend in this section, therefore, to strike out on our own, although we were impressed by Caplow and by Sisk (1977).

Cronbach, L.J. 1971. Test validation. In Thorndike, R.L. (Ed.), *Educational Measurement* (2nd ed.), 443-507. Washington D.C.: American Council on Education.

_____ 1983. *Designing Evaluations of Educational and Social Programs*. San Francisco: Jossey Bass.
— A basic reference setting out the variables and issues that need to be considered during the design and implementation of projects in programme evaluation.

Cutler, P. 1985. *Problem Solving in Clinical Medicine* (2nd ed.). Baltimore: Williams & Wilkins.
— One of the first texts organized in terms of body systems with the continuing theme of medical problem-solving.

Dyer, W.G. 1984. *Strategies for Managing Change*. Reading, Mass.: Addison-Wesley.

Ebel, R. 1979. *Essentials of Educational Measurement* (3rd ed.). Englewood Cliffs, NJ: Prentice-Hall.
— An authoritative source on principles and procedures of text construction.

Erickson, E.H. 1963. *Childhood and Society* (2nd ed.). New York: W.W.Norton.
— We are impressed by the similarity between the development of individuals, as described by Erikson, and the development of organizations. We invite others to make the same comparisons and to experiment so as to see if the parallel is useful in understanding human organizations, predicting their behaviour and controlling them.

Feinstein, A.R. 1967. *Clinical Judgment.* Baltimore: Williams & Wilkins.
— This classic in the early literature of problem-solving has as its theme the view that those judgements which physicians must make need to be backed by scientific concepts and principles applicable to medicine.

Fisher, L.A. & Levene, C. 1985. *Guide to the Educational Programme of the Faculty of Medicine, University of Calgary* (5th ed.). Calgary, Alberta: Faculty of Medicine.
— This handbook is designed to provide new faculty with the conceptual framework for understanding and applying the educational philosophy of the school.

Flanagan, J.C. 1954. The critical incident technique. *Psychol.Bull.* 51: 327-358.

Flexner, A. 1910. *Medical Education in the United States and Canada: A Report to the Carnegie Foundation for the Advancement of Teaching.* New York: Carnegie Foundation.
— For an interesting interpretation of Flexner's findings see Jonas (1978), 199-222.

Gagne, R.M. & Briggs, L.J. 1979. *Principles of Instructional Design* (2nd ed.). N.Y.: Holt, Rinehart & Winston.
— A thorough examination of modes of learning and of teaching, leading to principles of instructional design.

Gardner, J.W. 1965. *Self-renewal: the Individual and the Innovative Society.* New York: Harper & Row.
— Although an older book, it has not aged. It explores brilliantly the concept of renewal and the necessity of building the process into our individual and organizational lives.

Gregory, C.F. 1969. Orthopaedics and the impact of learning theory. *Journal of Medical Education*. *44*, No.9, 777-783.

Gronlund, N.E. 1985. *Stating Objectives for Classroom Instruction* (3rd ed.). New York: Macmillan.
— This book provides many examples of "action verbs" illustrating activities appropriate to different kinds of objectives.

Guba, E. & Lincoln, Y.S. 1982. *Effective Evaluation*. San Francisco: Jossey Bass.
— A book that can be read as a companion to the book on programme evaluation by Cronbach. It emphasizes the role of qualitative data and information in the conduct of meaningful, productive programme evaluation.

Ham, T.H. 1962. Medical education at Western Reserve University: A progress report for the sixteen years 194-662. *New England Journal of Medicine* 267: 868-874.
— One of the first open reports of the vicissitudes of curricular revision in a professional school.

Harrow, A.J. 1972. *A Taxonomy of the Psychomotor Domain*. New York: McKay.
— A companion book to the Bloom and Krathwohl taxonomies.

Hilgard, E.R. & Bower, G.H. 1981. *Theories of Learning* (5th ed.). Englewood Cliffs, N.J.: Prentice Hall.
— A most thorough overview of the different learning theories currently influencing research in the area.

Hubbard, J.P. 1978. *Measuring Medical Education* (2nd ed.). Philadelphia: Lea & Febiger.
— A standard reference on testing the acquisition of knowledge by the use of multiple-choice questions.

Johnson, D.W. & Johnson, F.P. 1982. *Joining Together: Group Theory and Group Skills* (2nd ed.). Englewood Cliffs, N.J.: Prentice-Hall.

Jonas, S. 1978. *Medical Mystery: the Training of Doctors in the United States*. New York: Norton.
— A commentary on current American medical curricula and their impact on students.

Keller, F.S. & Sherman, J.G. 1974. *The Keller Plan Handbook: Essays on a Personalized System of Instruction.* Menlo Park, CA.: Benjamin.

Kerlinger, F.M. 1973. *Foundations of Behavioral Research* (2nd ed.). New York: Holt, Rinehart & Winston.
— See Chapter 25: Foundations of measurement, and Chapter 31: Observations of behavior, for a further treatment of the particular problems associated with observation of student performance.

Krathwohl, D.R., Bloom, B.S. & Masia, B.B. 1964. *Taxonomy of Educational Objectives: Handbook II: Affective Domain.* New York: David McKay.

Lippard, V.W. 1974. *A Half-century of American Medical Education: 1920-1970.* New York: Josiah Macy Foundation.
— See Puschmann (1966) for the history of an earlier period.

Madaus, G.F., Scriven, M. & Stufflebeam, D.L. 1983. *Evaluation Models.* Boston: Kluwer-Nijhoff.
— A comprehensive overview of programme evaluation models in current use. A basic reference in the field.

Mager, R.F. 1975. *Preparing Instructional Objectives* (2nd ed.). Belmont, CA.: Fearon.
— A clear, useful aid in determining the most effective way of stating educational objectives.

McGuire, C. H., Solomon, L.M. & Forman, P.M. 1976. *Clinical Simulations* (2nd ed.). New York: Appleton Century Crofts.
— This book describes the construction, administration and interpretation of patient management problems.

McKeachie, W.J. 1986. *Teaching Tips* (8th ed.). Toronto: Heath.
— An excellent guide to effective teaching at the post-secondary level. For both beginning and experienced professional faculty the book discusses the many aspects of teaching that must be considered beyond possessing a solid understanding of one's own discipline.

Miller, G.E. (Ed.) 1961. *Teaching and Learning in Medical School.* Cambridge, Mass.: Harvard University Press.
— A book that provides a wide survey of principles and practices applicable to medical education.

_____ 1980. *Educating Medical Teachers.* Cambridge, Mass.: Harvard University Press.
— This book gives the most lucid description of the new emphasis in medical education. For a brilliant analysis of the current situation in North American medical schools see Chapter 10: Problems and Prospects.

Newble, D.I. & Cannon, R. 1987. *A Handbook for Medical Teachers* (2nd ed.). Lancaster, England: MTP Press.
— This book explores the different roles of a medical teacher, with an emphasis on clinical teaching. An excellent resource for the new or experienced clinician.

Petter, A. 1982. A closet within the house: learning objectives and the law school curriculum. In Gold, N. (Ed.) *Essays on Legal Education*, 77-96. Toronto: Butterworth & Co. (Canada) Limited.

Phi Delta Kappa. 1964. *Education and the Structure of Knowledge.* Chicago: Rand McNally.
— One of the first publications ever to study the relationship between content and structure of subject matter. In this summary of the proceedings of a symposium sponsored by Phi Delta Kappa, particular attention should be paid to J.J.Schwab: Problems, topics and issues, 443; and to D.P.Ausubel: Some psychological aspects of the structure of knowledge, 221-262.

Puschmann, T. 1966. *A History of Medical Education.* New York: Hafner. (A facsimile of the 1891 translation by Evan H. Hare.)
— A history of medical education up until the period preceding A. Flexner. See Lippard (1974) for recent American history.

Rogers, D.E. 1980. On preparing academic health centers for the very different 1980s. *Journal of Medical Education.* 55, 112.
— A current commentary on problems of medical centres in the United States.

Rossi, P.H. & Freeman, H.E. 1985. *Evaluation: a Systematic Approach* (3rd ed.). Beverly Hills, CA: Sage Publications.
— A beautifully detailed book on principles and procedures of programme evaluation. Illustrative examples are frequent and succinct.

Schwab, J.J. 1969. *College Curriculum and Student Protest.* Chicago: University of Chicago Press.
— A fine analysis of the general impact of student unrest in the colleges.

Sisk, H.L.   1977. *Management and Organization* (3rd ed.).   Cincinatti, Ohio: South-Western.

Skinner, B.F.   1968.   *The Technology of Teaching.*   New York: Meredith.
— This work gives the flavour of the behaviourist movement in education. The book is far more than its title implies, being Skinner's rationale for the development of a theory of learning and, consequently, a theory of instruction.

Southern Illinois University School of Medicine.   1980. *Curricular Objectives.*   Springfield, Ill.: Southern Illinois University.
— A rather heroic compilation of objectives for a medical school curriculum.   It demonstrates what can be done if a professional faculty adheres unswervingly to a goal and a set of principles and procedures for writing objectives.   The work is organized by study units and modules of instruction, with an overview of the process of local curriculum planning given at the beginning of the book.

Stevens, S.S.   1974. Measurement. In Maranell, G.M. (Ed.)   *Scaling: a Source Book for Behavioral Scientists,* 22-41. Chicago: Aldine.

Tyler, R.W.   1949.   *Basic Principles of Curriculum and Instruction.* Chicago: University of Chicago Press.
— An excellent approach to learning and instruction from the viewpoint of a curriculum consultant.   This treatise has been in print for almost forty years without losing any of its utility for curriculum planners.   A good book for introducing curricular theory to the uninitiated faculty member in a professional school.

Wakeford, R. (Ed.) 1985. *Proceedings of the First Cambridge Conference on Clinical Competence.*   Cambridge: Cambridge University Press.

Webb, E.J., Campbell, D.T., Schwartz, R.F. & Sechrest, L.   1966. *Unobtrusive Measures: Nonreactive Research in the Social Sciences.* Chicago: Rand McNally.
— This book provides some imaginative thinking on observation of performance in general, and has intriguing suggestions for collecting data on performance with minimal impact on the subject under study.

INDEX

DATE DUE